RACHEL
GUNN

IMPACT
PARENTING

PRINCIPLES FOR CULTIVATING A HEALTHY HOME

This book is intended to offer thoughtful insight and encouragement. While the book provides practical, research-backed principles and relatable stories to guide you, it is not intended to replace professional counseling or advice. Always seek the guidance of qualified professionals for specific concerns or issues.

Published by MOMCO, LLC

Library of Congress Control Number: 2024913917

Paperback ISBN: 979-8-9909522-0-1

E-Book ISBN: 979-8-9909522-2-5

www.rachelgunn.com

To Brent, my biggest supporter and champion.
My future and forever response to "You think you're an expert?"
will be, "Well, I did write the book."

To my daughters. Thank you for making me look good
and letting me put your business on the streets.

Katelyn, thank you for being the beta child.
Please don't send me to the nursing home.

Sarah, thank you for challenging my ideas about parenting.
I'm glad you're not Melvin.

FORWARD

I am the director of a non-profit organization that houses, feeds, counsels, and educates displaced women and their children in critical moments of their lives. Many of our mothers are coming out of incarceration, addiction, and homelessness. Many are desperate for realistic parenting guidance to help them raise their children without guilt or fear. When Rachel showed up at our door with some parenting expertise and a heart to serve, we were excited to have her share her knowledge with our moms.

She has served for several years, teaching our ladies this material. It has made such a tremendous impact: building confidence where there had been none, equipping mothers with skills and methods when they have felt completely unequipped, and empowering our mothers with the ability to empower their children, who, until now, all have felt powerless. I am thrilled that she has finally put it all down in a book so everyone can have access to her parenting principles.

Impact Parenting is a phenomenal tool for all parents! It is a must-read for anyone who desires to parent with an everlasting impact. Like Rachel's mother, I wish I had this book while raising my children. It has so much valuable information laid out so that it is easy to understand and apply. The format makes it applicable and practical to do as a small group or by yourself.

Rachel's passion, kindness, and talents are evident in her teachings and throughout this book. She has a God-given anointing, and it shines through this material. No matter your social status, if you are a parent, grandparent, or even part of a child's life, this book is for you.

Melinda MeGahee
Executive Director, The Lovelady Center

A NOTE TO THE READER

I know a lot about parenting. From research. From education. From experience. I have learned a lot in my efforts to be the best parent I can for my daughters. I also know that I don't know everything.

From my experience as a mom, I know that parenting is personal and emotional. Fear of judgment is a real thing when it comes to our parenting.

From my experience as an educator, I know there is no single right or wrong way to parent.

While I know some things (not all) about parenting, I don't know your kids, your family, or your situation. Only you know what works and doesn't work for your family. As parents, we can and should seek advice from those we trust, but we should also learn to listen to and trust our instincts when it comes to our children. Not everything works for everyone.

As you read this book, I encourage you to do two things.

First, reflect on yourself as a parent. This can be difficult because, as we know, parenting can be very emotional. I have found myself in tears seeing my daughters make choices that went completely against everything I believed I had taught and modeled for them. My decisions have been questioned and challenged by my own children (and they were right!). It is hard. I get it. But try to be open to self-exploration as you read.

Second, listen to your instincts. God gave us instincts to protect us and our children. Be confident in your place as their parent. You know yourself, your children, and your family. If you come across something you know won't work for your family, it's okay to let it go and move on to something else. It's that simple, especially if you are working on self-reflection.

Remember that parenting is a journey marked by learning and growth. While I have gained substantial knowledge from research, education, and personal experience, I understand that every family is unique. My insights may provide guidance, but ultimately, you know your children and family dynamics best. Seek advice, trust your instincts, and adapt strategies to fit your family's needs. Embrace self-reflection and listen to your inner voice. This journey is about discovering what works best for you and your children and fostering a nurturing environment where they can thrive.

Rachel

Prepare your child for the path, instead of the path for your child.

Tim Elmore

TABLE OF CONTENTS

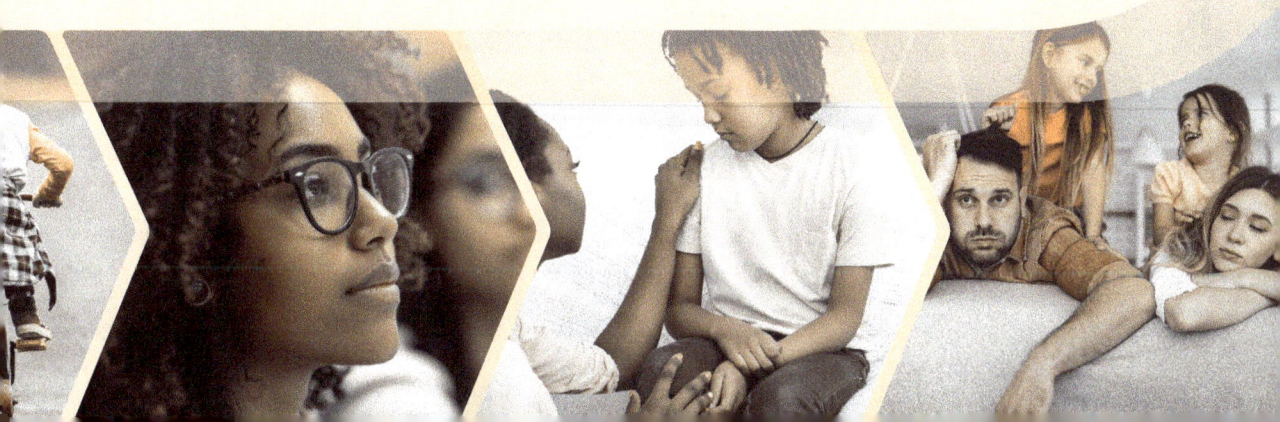

INTRODUCTION

INTRODUCTION

When my children were in elementary school, I went out of town with a friend. We stopped along the way to visit another friend and spend the night. We woke up around six the next morning and found our friend in the kitchen, fully dressed. She had prepared a wonderful breakfast, and when we asked her about it, she said, "I do this every morning. I just want my kids to feel well-received."

I immediately felt ashamed of my own shortcomings in the mornings. Breakfast for my kids consisted mostly of what they could make for themselves: cereal, toast, breakfast bars, etc. When I got home, I tried to start making breakfast for my daughters. The first morning, I woke up early and made a fabulous feast. When they came down, they were surprised and delighted! After a couple of days, though, I realized that they weren't actually eating the breakfast I made. They would pick at it, then politely ask for a frozen waffle. I realized why I didn't make breakfast for my kids: they didn't eat it. And that early in the morning, I didn't want to fight with them about it. I felt like a failure as a mom.

I continued to ponder this, wondering what I was doing to make my kids feel "well-received." It didn't take long to come up with my list. I make it a point to stay off my phone when my kids are in the car. If I am chatting when they get in, I end the call. I put notes in their lunchboxes. We eat dinner together and listen to their stories about their days. I lie down with each of them in the evenings before bed and give them my full attention for 10-15 minutes. When we talk, I give them my full attention. I make myself available to drive them to their friends' houses, and I never make them feel bad about it. I create a safe space for family time in the evenings.

After really thinking about it, I realized that I didn't fall short in making my kids feel well-received—I just did it differently than other moms.

As a teacher, I realized that discipline isn't just about enforcing rules and doling out consequences—it is a nuanced approach to guiding young minds toward understanding the broader implications of their actions. This realization hit home when I had kids of my own. Navigating the challenges of raising my own children helped me grasp the delicate balance between setting boundaries and nurturing our children's growth.

In 2014, I quit teaching to be home with my children and quickly found myself meeting moms for coffee and helping them navigate their own parenting struggles. Soon this "coffee talk ministry" grew into something more: a journey that led me to work with parents professionally and to eventually write this book. With a unique perspective as both a parent and educator, I have personally encountered the profound love and protective instincts that come with parenthood, while also possessing the ability, as a teacher, to recognize a child's potential and foster their growth. I'm excited to pour these perspectives into the pages of this book and I hope they will resonate with you as you face similar joys and dilemmas.

As parents, we are the experts on our children, and we should also seek wisdom and insight from those in our trusted circle. But we should always seek the Lord first and foremost.[1] As followers of Christ, our first step should be to lean into God's Word and seek the Holy Spirit, which He gave us and who will guide us in truth. As you read and work through this book, be mindful of the principles and strategies, but always filter them through your God-given instincts about what is best for your family.

My prayer is that in this book you will find valuable principles, hope, and encouragement that will guide and equip you in your role as a parent.

---

1   Matthew 6:33

MAKING THE MOST OF THIS BOOK

There is no one-size-fits-all approach to parenting.

The goal of this book is to guide you through various stages of parenting, equipping you with well-established, healthy principles that have been proven to have a positive impact. Ideally, you can apply these principles in your daily parenting, finding them practical and effective in various situations. These principles are rooted in extensive research and widely recognized as beneficial, offering a dependable and well-founded approach to nurturing your child's growth and well-being.

However, within these pages, you'll discover much more than just principles. I've woven stories from my own experiences as a mother and those shared with me by fellow parents. My hope is that you will not only learn new principles but also connect with the raw, rewarding journey of parenting itself. By sharing personal anecdotes and insights, I strive to make this book not just informative but relatable, creating a connection that goes beyond the pages and speaks directly to your experiences as a parent.

CHAPTER GUIDE

In Chapter 1, we'll dive into some essential parenting foundations that lay the groundwork for the entire book. Chapters 2 through 4 are where we'll explore the various stages of parenting based on a child's age and development. We will break down the boundaries, teaching, and nurturing stages, covering ages one through eighteen. For each stage of parenting, we will explore characteristics of healthy communication, connection, and correction.

Moving on to Chapter 5, we'll shift our focus to parenting a child who has experienced trauma. Understanding the effects of trauma is a crucial part of providing the support our children need during their recovery journey. In the final chapter, "The Family Reset," we'll talk about resetting. While the goal of Impact Parenting is to start early and build foundations, it's okay if you are starting later. "The Family Reset" will walk you through discovering the problems, exploring their root causes, and creating a plan to reset and begin fostering healthy relationships.

While this book covers parenting through stages, almost everything you learn throughout these pages can be applied at any time as a parent. So whether you are a parent of toddlers or teens, you will find the principles applicable to your parenting. Learning the principles of setting and holding boundaries for toddlers will help parents of teens understand and apply the principles found in Chapter 4, "The Teen Years." In the same way, the principles found in Chapter 4 will help new parents begin planting seeds that will produce a healthy harvest during the teen years.

This book is designed to encourage critical thinking because there is no one-size-fits-all approach to parenting. As you read, I recommend keeping a pen handy. Feel free to jot down notes in the margins, underline, and star the ideas that resonate with you. This way, as you navigate the different stages of parenthood, you can return to this book year after year to find valuable insights. The stories shared within may remind you of your own experiences and offer practical applications of the principles discussed. Be sure to jot them down as little reminders to revisit these pages whenever you need them.

THINK AND DISCUSS

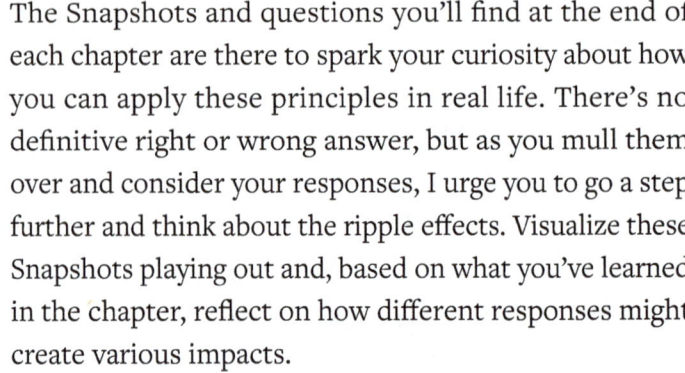

The Snapshots and questions you'll find at the end of each chapter are there to spark your curiosity about how you can apply these principles in real life. There's no definitive right or wrong answer, but as you mull them over and consider your responses, I urge you to go a step further and think about the ripple effects. Visualize these Snapshots playing out and, based on what you've learned in the chapter, reflect on how different responses might create various impacts.

If you are using this book with a small group, you'll have a fantastic opportunity for some meaningful discussions! Sharing thoughts and ideas in a group can open up new perspectives beyond our own experiences, and that's where real learning and growth happen. So, ensure the discussion is open and supportive, creating an environment that encourages everyone to participate and learn from each other.

For clarity and consistency, I have used two couples for the Snapshots: Adam and Priscilla and Jason and Charlotte. Neither couple represents a certain type of parenting. They are used interchangeably throughout the Snapshots.

SELF-REFLECTION

These questions are meant to guide you through a personal reflection of your parenting journey, from where you have been to where you are going. They encourage self-awareness and self-improvement, serving as a guide on your parenting path. By honestly examining your past experiences and your present parenting approach, you can gain valuable insights that will empower you to make intentional choices as you move forward in your parenting journey. These questions invite you to take a deeper look within yourself, promoting personal growth and a stronger, more connected relationship with your children.

As you read and reflect on the questions here, I want to remind you to approach them with an open mind and a non-judgmental heart. The purpose here isn't to open wounds or invite feelings of shame, but rather to explore ourselves and foster understanding and growth. We have all been shaped by our past experiences, and many of us carry the weight of difficult backgrounds. Add to that the deeply personal journey of parenting, and we can find ourselves feeling overwhelmed with many different emotions.

As you reflect on your own parenting, please be gentle with yourself. It's natural to stumble upon aspects of ourselves that we wish were different, but even then, kindness towards ourselves is paramount. Embracing this compassionate approach opens the door to rewriting behaviors, paving the way for profound personal growth and transformation. So, as you reflect, do so with tenderness and understanding, knowing that each step forward is a testament to your resilience and strength.

I'm excited to share this valuable information and encourage you as you navigate the incredible journey of parenthood.

1

PARENTING FOUNDATIONS

PARENTING FOUNDATIONS

I wish my parents had known this.

I *wish my parents had known this.* This has, by far, been the most common response to this book. In fact, my mom, who was my sounding board throughout writing this book, said the same about herself. She wished that she had information like this when she was raising my siblings and me. Unfortunately, parenting for so many of our parents, and for us, has felt like walking through a minefield. We never know what's coming, and all we can do is lick our wounds when things blow up.

This chapter holds the first step toward finding a roadmap that will help us navigate the journey with more confidence and less guesswork. Understanding foundational principles of parenting will help us handle whatever twists and turns are thrown our way. These foundations will help us adapt to our children's unique personalities and evolving needs. Plus, knowing the ropes gives you the freedom to adapt and make choices that suit your family's unique style and needs.

FOUNDATION 1: IMPULSE VS. IMPACT PARENTING

Parenting is incredibly fluid. It is also unique and personal; the culture within a home takes on the blended personalities of the parents. Most parents would not even realize that the impulse and impact parenting approaches exist. We just parent the best way we know, usually by accepting or rejecting the ways of our parents. As you read the following descriptions, you will likely relate more to one or the other. If you relate more to Impact Parenting, you will probably agree with most of what you read in this book and will find insights into using the relationship you've built as your kids transition into young adults. If you relate more to Impulse Parenting, don't worry—you are in the right place! You will learn principles that can help you build a strong relationship with your kids. As you strengthen that relationship, you will notice your stress levels decreasing and your home becoming more peaceful.

These are not absolutes, and we most likely won't see all of these characteristics in any one home. These descriptions will give us an idea of the different characteristics that may be present in each home. Let's consider the differences as we look at the Impact and Impulse parenting homes.

WHEN IMPULSE RULES

The impulse home tends to be more present-focused, reacting to situations as they arise. The parents in this home may find themselves caught off guard a good bit. Their reactions to their kids' antics tend to be more emotional. They may also find themselves constantly putting out fires, which can be tiresome and draining. In homes where impulse rules, we often see parents who are stressed, burnt out, and looking around for ways to get away from it all.

The kids in a home where impulse rules tend to have some sort of power over the parents. This may be that they get their way when they argue, cry, pitch a fit, or manipulate in some way. They tend to react emotionally to change, especially when things don't go their way. These kids might start having problems in school. Parents may receive notes, emails, or calls about discipline issues. These kids often struggle with following classroom rules and meeting social etiquette standards. Parents struggle to deal with these issues and this can often create a negative cycle within the home. The child builds a discipline profile at school, the school contacts parents, something has to be done, parents react emotionally, the child tries to walk the straight and narrow for a while, and then the cycle restarts. Children from these homes tend to have less self-awareness and self-confidence.

WHEN IMPACT RULES

In homes where impact rules, we often see parents who, while stressed, are not over-whelmed with the job of parenting. They understand that parenting comes with many difficult situations and seasons. They use structure and boundaries to create peace in the home. They understand that the decisions they make today will impact the future culture of their home. They set boundaries and establish their authority early, paving the way for building a strong relationship with their kids. They often consider the future and what it will bring for their kids and prepare so that they can respond in a way that will foster the healthiest dynamic within the family. Rather than put out fires, they know the path they want to take and are guided by their goals as parents. They are proactive in dealing with problems and behaviors that arise, looking for patterns and signs that something is amiss. They respond to their kids' antics in a more objective way, taking in all the information before making decisions. While these parents at times still need a break, it comes more from a place of self-care than a grasp for sanity.

Kids who come from a home where impact rules tend to be aware of their position in the home. They understand that, while they are loved, they are not in charge. They tend to respond well to change and cope well when things do not go their way. These kids tend to excel in school and are described as leaders by their teachers. When a problem does arise at school, their parents are often aware before the school notifies them. They generally deal with these issues in a way that helps their child learn a life lesson and move forward in a positive direction. Children from these homes tend to have more self-awareness and self-confidence

REACTING VS. RESPONDING

As we've learned, reacting is a major characteristic of impulse parenting and is mostly about how a parent is feeling in the moment. Responding falls in line with impact parenting and is geared towards finding a resolution and teaching through life experience.

We've all been there—saying something in the moment to our child that we immediately (or later) regret. It's bound to happen as our kids start exploring more of their world—we'll be caught off guard by some of the things they do, and we won't always react positively. It is not the end of the world; we apologize and try to do better. For now, we are focusing on the "doing better" part. Part of building a stronger relationship is making sure that we are a safe place for our kids. This means that we work to make sure that our kids feel comfortable coming to us with their questions and that they feel comfortable making mistakes around us.

Our reactions often come from our own unmet needs—emotional landmines that our kids unknowingly step on. A key part of learning to respond as a parent is understanding our own emotional needs and working to have them met. But sometimes our reactions are just a lack of self-control. As parents, we must learn to control our actions when emotions are running high. While this can be a tough task, the more we practice, the easier it will become, and it will make a world of difference in relating to your child.

As a young mom, reacting emotionally was a big struggle for me. It wasn't until I realized the negative impact my outbursts had on my children that I began to realize the importance of controlling my temper and my actions. Breaking habits like this isn't always easy, and it takes both time and the realization that there's a more positive approach to fostering a healthier relationship with our children.

As my kids grew older and I modeled self-control, I also shared about the difficulties of having to learn this as an adult. This transparency gave them a look into the heart behind why it is so important to control themselves in times of big emotions.

This doesn't mean that we can't be angry or sad or frustrated. It just means that we need to work on how we respond during those emotional moments. We are accountable for our actions, and we can't use our emotions as an excuse!

THE POWER OF THE PAUSE

We all have wisdom in us, but sometimes, we allow our emotional reactions to take over! Let's face it; when it comes to our kids, there is no limit to the wild antics, crazy situations, and outrageous acts of childhood we might face. Of course, we know we should be slow to anger, but what about when our kids have splintered our last nerve? When they have been arguing for the last four hours? When they use our own words against us (and they are right)? Sometimes it is just plain hard to stay calm. We find ourselves in moments of shock, and we tend to let our emotions take over.

Taking a pause gives us space to calm down and control those negative reactions. The pause is a powerful tool, allowing us a moment to change directions. If we train ourselves to pause before we speak or react in most situations, we will find that our responses are more measured and wise. We can let the negative, emotion-driven reactions go and begin to replace them with more thoughtful responses.

Responding allows us to consider the long-term effects of a situation and the needs of our children. It allows us to gather information rather than make assumptions. It helps us create a safe space for our children to make mistakes and learn from them. In the long run, responding can help influence our kids to be more open with us about their struggles when they are teens. How we respond to the little things tells them how we will respond to the big things.

> The pause is a powerful tool, allowing us a moment to change directions.

"Know this, my beloved brothers: let every person be quick to hear, slow to speak, slow to anger; for the anger of man does not produce the righteousness of God."

James 1:19–20 (ESV)

Pausing is a great tool to disrupt our reactive responses. We can also go a step further and explore our reactions to understand where they are coming from and decrease our emotional responses.

THE FACT CHECK

The FACT Check is a simple framework for assessing our emotional reactions. When we recognize those emotions rising up in us and take a pause, we can go through these simple steps to help us find the root of our frustration.

F
FEELINGS
What am I feeling right now?

A
ACTIONS
What is happening to make me feel this way?

C
CORRECT
Are my feelings correct?

T
TRUTH
What is the truth about this situation?

F = Feelings

The F in FACT check means we identify our feelings. So when we first *feel* those feelings, we can take a second to identify them. As we begin to recognize our feelings, it will become easier to identify them in those brief moments right before we explode. We might be surprised that anger is not actually what we are experiencing. What first feels like anger could be hurt, embarrassment, stress, anxiety, or frustration.

It took a long time and a lot of practice, but I have learned over the years that when I start to feel hot, or flushed, it means I am having some big emotions. Now that I know that feeling, I have learned to stop and think whenever I feel it. It has kept me from reacting (or overreacting) on many occasions. I have found that when I can recognize and reflect on that initial feeling, I can shift directions toward a more positive outcome with my children.

A = Actions

Once we have identified our feelings, we move to identify the action. What has happened that caused us to feel this way? Did our kids do something wrong? Was it something that happened earlier in the day? Something we know will be happening later? When we take the time to think about why we are actually upset, we might be surprised, again, to realize that the cause is not what we were thinking.

When I began reflecting in heated moments, I found more times than I cared to admit that I was angry because I felt I had lost control of the situation. I had given into begging or been sucked into an argument, defending myself from a seven-year-old. I cannot count the times I went back into my daughter's room after I had declared it bedtime and I would not be back. When I learned to examine the situation more closely, I began to realize that many times I was angry at the situation, or even at myself.

C = Correct

Once we know what we are feeling and why, we can begin to consider whether or not the feeling is correct. We can ask ourselves, is my feeling in line with the situation? Are my feelings directed at the right person or event? The more we evaluate our feelings, the better we will become at changing our emotional reactions into thoughtful responses.

Thinking back to those bedtime battles, I can see that my anger and frustration came from feeling like I had lost control of the situation. That wasn't my child's fault. Honestly, I don't even blame my younger mom-self. I didn't have the knowledge or the tools to handle a toddler who was trying to find her own way in the world. When I understood that my daughters and I were all just inexperienced, it helped me focus more on learning to navigate bedtimes and take a calmer approach.

T = Truth

Now we can ask ourselves, what is the truth? Whether we are asking about a practical or biblical truth, it's valuable to take this step. Identifying our mixed-up or misplaced emotions can be helpful, but identifying the truth of these situations can help us break these emotional cycles in the future. Over time, as we identify the lies that lead to our emotional reactions and the truths that counteract those lies, we will find that it becomes easier to dismiss the lie, go straight to the truth, and avoid reactions altogether.

My daughters and I had been out running errands all day and I wanted takeout from a certain restaurant. I offered to get them something as well. My younger daughter asked if she could get something from a nearby restaurant. It was not too far out of the way so I said yes. Then my oldest daughter asked to get something from another restaurant that was farther out of the way. I was frustrated because I didn't want to go that far, but I had already said yes to the first daughter. I told them if they could agree on one restaurant, we would get it. They could not agree.

More frustrated, I turned around and went to get dinner from the faraway restaurant. As we headed back to the original place, it started to rain. With no drive-thru, this meant I would be getting wet. I began to snap at my daughters about how they couldn't just be happy with what they were offered. I was so frustrated and as I was talking, I looked at them and realized that I needed to rethink my attitude.

Take a look at this situation using the FACT check.

I identified my FEELING as frustration. I was just plain frustrated that I had to go to three different restaurants. I was tired and cranky (two more feelings) and ready to be home. I identified the ACTION as my own. I had offered them something then said yes when they asked for something else. I had created the situation. I identified that while my feeling was CORRECT, I was blaming them for it, which was not correct. They didn't do anything wrong. Then, I identified the TRUTH: I was frustrated at the situation I had created, and I was taking it out on them.

When I communicated this with them and apologized for it, the tension in the car melted. Not only did they feel more secure knowing that I was not angry with them, but it also eased my frustration. Just getting it out (saying it out loud) helped, and I was able to turn my mood around.

Reacting is a part of life. Even the most level-headed of us will react from time to time. That's okay. The important thing is that we are aware of our emotions and our reactions and that we continue to work at becoming responders.

SELF-REFLECTION

Reflect on your recent parenting experiences. What are some moments when you reacted emotionally or responded thoughtfully? What triggered your reactions? What, if anything, helped you respond thoughtfully? How did your child respond in each circumstance?

....

....

....

....

....

....

....

FOUNDATION 2: STAGES OF PARENTING

NURTURING STAGE
Birth to Age 1

1

During this time a baby needs to know that he or she is safe. Our job is to create a safe space for our child and meet all his or her needs.

TEACHING STAGE
Ages 5 to 11

3

Our children will be FULL of questions; more that we can imagine! Answer them! Give them the "why" behind the "what."

BOUNDARIES STAGE
Ages 1 to 5

2

Children start to test boundaries. We will need to set clear boundaries and establish ourselves as their authority.

COACHING STAGE
Ages 12 to 17

4

Our children will begin to seek independence. We give strategic freedoms and allow them to suffer the consequences of bad decisions.

MENTORING STAGE
Ages 18 to 25

5

Our children will need our help and advice often as they grow and mature. Give advice only when asked and withold judgement.

FRIENDSHIP STAGE
Adulthood

6

Our children become more like peers. They are independent, and we are able to enjoy each other's company as adults.

In 1981, Ellen Galinsky proposed six stages of parenting that were based on child development.[1] Over the years, many parenting experts have developed versions of the parenting stages. This six-stage model is based on Galinsky's original.

NURTURING STAGE: Birth to about 1 year

During this time a baby is dependent on us for everything, and they need to know that they are safe. When we create a safe space for our children and meet all their needs, we help them develop a secure attachment, which is important to their development.

BOUNDARIES STAGE: Ages 1 to 5

This is the time when children start to test boundaries. It is okay and even natural for them to do this. During this time, we will need to set clear and consistent boundaries and establish ourselves as their authority. It can be tempting to allow them to run free, but this can create struggles down the road. Boundaries help children feel safe as they explore the world around them.

TEACHING STAGE: Ages 6 to 11

In this stage of parenting, we begin to teach the heart of our children. They will be FULL of questions (more than we can imagine)! Answer them! This is the time that we give our children the "why" behind the "what." During

When we know where we are, we know what to expect.

---

1   Galinsky, E. (1987) *The Six Stages of Parenthood*. Reading, MA: Perseus Books

this time, our connection with our children will begin to move away from the physical and become more relational.

COACHING STAGE: Ages 12 to 18

This is the stage of parenting where we should step back and allow our children to take ownership of some of their decisions. We begin to take the role of coach–giving advice while allowing our teens to make the ultimate decision. We should also allow our kids to experience the consequences of their decisions. During this stage our parenting moves from rules and consequences to influence and conversations.

MENTORING STAGE: 18 to Early Adulthood

Once our kids are 18 or older, they should be living their lives. Our adult children will often need our help and advice as they grow and mature. We should strive to be the mentors they need, giving advice only when asked. We should reassure our children through their early adulthood and avoid judging their decisions.

FRIENDSHIP STAGE: Adulthood

Our children become more like peers. They are independent and you are able to enjoy each other's company as adults. We are no longer their parents in the same sense that we were. A former president will always be known by the office and receive the honors of the office, but he no longer has the power of the office. As parents, we will always hold the title and place of honor, but we should no longer hold or try to wield power over our children.

Knowing the stages of parenting can help us understand where we are in the parenting process. We don't have to wonder about how to best parent our kids—we can parent with a plan!

SELF-REFLECTION

What stage is each of your children in? Based on that stage, what does each child need most from you right now?

....

....

....

....

....

....

....

FOUNDATION 3: PARENTING STYLES

You may have heard of different parenting styles, (which one is best, which to avoid, etc.). But our parenting style simply refers to how we relate to and interact with our children. Some of us are more lenient, allowing our kids to make their own decisions, while others are more strict, utilizing rules and consequences. There are many different combinations of styles and we usually go back and forth between styles depending on our moods and the situation. As we learn more about each style and identify our own tendencies, remember to see this as an opportunity to learn and grow—regardless of where you currently find yourself.

We all have ideas about what parenting should look like. For many of us, these ideas come from our own parents. Despite our professions that we would never do the things our parents did, most of us have realized at one time or another that we are doing exactly what our parents did. As parents, we have a tremendous amount of influence over our children (both positive and negative) whether we are trying or not. And whether we embrace or reject the way our parents raised us, our own parenting style is inevitably influenced by them.

As we explore styles, you may relate to one more than the others. Keep in mind that parents don't usually fall strictly into one style or another. While it's common to find ourselves relating more to one style, most of us show tendencies from each one depending on the situation. Our goal isn't to put ourselves in a box but to learn more about our styles so we can grow as parents.

While there are many parenting styles, for our purposes, we'll focus on three main ones: Permissive, Authoritarian, and Authoritative. As you read through these descriptions, you will likely relate to one style more than the others. That is your main parenting style.

Permissive (▲ Relationship, ▼ Rules)

Permissive parents tend to take on more of a friendship role than a parental one. They are often lenient, only stepping in when there's a serious problem. This type of parent is quite forgiving and will generally give in if a child begs for something. Permissive parents typically don't put as much effort into discouraging poor choices or bad behavior. These parents encourage their children to talk with them about their issues. While their children will usually open up to them, they tend to find other sources for advice.

It's important to understand that permissive parenting has its merits, such as fostering open communication and independence in children. However, there's a flip side. This parenting style can sometimes cause parents to miss the opportunity to instill essential life skills, create structure, and guide children in making well-rounded choices.

Authoritarian (▲ Rules, ▼ Relationship)

Authoritarian parents are high on rules and low on relationships. They tend to be more strict, often focusing on making sure rules are followed with few or no exceptions. Authoritarian parents usually expect total obedience from their children and may use punishment(s) as a way of ensuring obedience. Rather than taking the time to teach their children how to make better choices, they tend to punish them for their mistakes. Authoritarian parents usually don't involve their children in problem-solving challenges. As a result, children of authoritarian parents do not usually open up to them and will also tend to find other sources for advice.

The authoritarian parenting style has its share of both commendable and less desirable aspects. On one hand, it thrives on structure and discipline, setting clear boundaries for children. The unwavering expectations for obedience can instill a sense of responsibility and an understanding of the importance of rules. This approach often ensures that children are aware of consequences and the need to follow instructions diligently.

However, the stringent approach of authoritarian parenting may sometimes overshadow the nurturing of a warm, empathetic parent-child relationship. The demand for obedience can lead to fear of consequences rather than an understanding of making sound choices.

The exclusion of children from problem-solving challenges can result in a lack of engagement and cooperation.

Authoritative (Relationship + Rules)

Authoritative parents tend to have rules and use consequences, but they also value teaching and listening. They find a healthy balance between rules and relationships, validating their children's feelings while also making it clear that the final decision rests with them. Authoritative parents invest time and energy into teaching appropriate behaviors and use positive discipline to reinforce good behavior. Children of authoritative parents tend to open up to their parents and also seek their advice and wisdom. This style is widely believed to be the most beneficial to children.

Finding the right balance between being a friend and being a parent is a delicate, yet crucial, task. Ultimately, effective parenting is about discovering that balance, ensuring children grow with both freedom and guidance while nurturing their individuality and independence. It's a journey that celebrates the unique individuality and growing independence of each child, all while nurturing the parent-child bond that's at the heart of their growth and development.

To help you identify your parenting style, you can take a short quiz found on the following page.

Finding the right balance between being a friend and being a parent is a delicate, yet crucial, task.

SELF-REFLECTION

Reflect on how your own upbringing and experiences with your parents may be influencing your current parenting style. In what ways are you embracing or rejecting the parenting techniques you experienced as a child? How has this influenced your parenting journey?

....

....

....

....

....

....

....

QUIZ[1]: WHAT IS YOUR PARENTING STYLE?

Read each statement below and circle the letter of the ones that best describe your current parenting beliefs or actions. (Remember, there are no wrong answers!)

B I am in control and I expect my kids to understand that and do as I say.

A It is better to give a little ground and protect the peace than to stand firm and provoke a fight.

C I have high expectations, but I work with my kids to help them meet those expectations.

B Too many children today talk back to their parents when they should just obey their parents.

A If my kids are unhappy with the situation, I try to find a way to make them happy.

C It is better if kids know the consequences before they break the rules.

B I was spanked when I was a child, and I turned out okay.

C When I give my child a task or job, I take the time to make sure he understands what to do.

B Children need discipline that hurts a little so that they will remember the lesson later.

A I don't give consequences when my kids don't mind, I just ask them to try harder next time.

C Sometimes when children talk, they make good points so I try to listen to them.

B My children should do as I say until they are old enough to move out and make their own decisions.

C Although it takes hard work, parents and children should try to talk about their feelings to make family decisions.

B When my children don't mind me, I yell at them or threaten them with punishment.

C It is okay for kids to question my rules and decisions, as long as they are respectful.

---

1   Quiz adapted from https://activeparenting.com/for-parents/parenting-quiz/

A If parents provide a good environment, children will pretty much raise themselves.

C Children should be allowed to be individuals. Their opinions matter.

A My child has no regular chores around the home but will occasionally pitch in when asked.

B My child gets a spanking at least once a month.

A If you let children have pretty free rein, they will eventually learn appropriate behaviors from the consequences of their actions.

B I am the parent, and I expect my children to conform to my decisions without discussion.

A I wish my child wouldn't interrupt my conversations so often.

C I do not criticize my children or call them names even when I can't understand why they act as they do.

A I feel best about my parenting when my kids are happy.

B I have to threaten my child with punishment at least once a week.

C Children shouldn't always get their way, but we ought to learn to listen to what they have to say.

A Whether we like it or not, children have the last word about what they will or won't do.

C We have discussed chores at our home and everybody takes part.

→ Count the number of As, Bs, and Cs you circled, and write the number next to each letter below.

How many of each letter did you circle?   A _____   B _____   C _____

A = Permissive   B = Authoritarian   C = Authoritative

The quiz and your results are not scientific—they are only meant to make you aware of your current views toward parenting. Regardless of which style you relate to the most, we can all use this knowledge going forward as we build stronger, healthier relationships with our kids!

FOUNDATION 4:
POWER OVER VS. POWER WITH

The real goal of parenting is not to control our children but to lend our support and guidance as they learn to control themselves.

There is an important power dynamic in the parent-child relationship. If we establish our authority in the boundaries stage, then we hold the power. If we do not, then our children likely do. When our children have the power, we usually find ourselves putting out fires and resorting to impulse parenting. When parents have the power, then we have a choice: use our power over our children or use it with our children.

We need to thoughtfully consider the idea of wielding power over versus with our children because this concept will deeply affect our children and our relationship with them. Power over relies on control to get our kids to obey us. Power with relies on empowerment to get our kids to problem-solve and take responsibility for their actions. Power over is commonly seen in authoritarian parenting, while power with is found commonly in the authoritative style.

When we have the power-over mindset, we tend to give orders and directives and expect obedience without question. This way of thinking is most often seen in the authoritarian style of parenting. However, using power over our children takes away their autonomy and stifles their confidence. In many cases, it often breeds resentment as children grow older and seek independence.

Authority in parenting does not mean that we control our kids. While we work with our kids to equip them to solve problems and make wise decisions, we still have the final word in decision-making. Rather than just telling our kids what to do and how to act, we teach them and empower them to take personal responsibility. While we are establishing our authority in the boundaries stage, we should work with our toddlers to show them the boundaries and help them understand that the authority rests with us.

As our kids head into the teaching stage, the difference between power over and power with becomes more recognizable. We are teachers, guides, and protectors of our children, not dictators. Power with means we lend them our wisdom, guide them to make good choices and help them through the consequences of their bad choices.

The real goal of parenting is not to control our children but to lend our support and guidance as they learn to control themselves.

USING POWER OVER CHILDREN

Using power over children can take many forms, all of which can have negative effects on our children's emotional well-being and development. One form is punishing a child without any explanation or discussion. Using both physical and emotional punishment without helping our children understand why they are being punished is more likely to instill doubt and fear than to help them correct their behaviors. This approach can leave children feeling bewildered and apprehensive without any real learning taking place.

Another form involves creating rules without seeking input from our child, which can make them feel disempowered and undervalued, potentially leading to rebellious behavior. In the same way, ignoring our children's feelings and opinions when making decisions can also make them feel insignificant and unheard. When our children feel as if they are unseen and unheard it can often lead to attention-seeking and sometimes rebellious behaviors.

Using physical force or threats to control a child's behavior can instill fear and cause long-term emotional and psychological harm. When we make threats or use force to control our children, it creates a hostile environment that undermines their emotional well-being. Beyond the immediate impact, it can inflict lasting emotional scars.

These approaches ultimately compromise the parent-child relationship and impede the child's growth. Let's aim for a more nurturing and empathetic approach that fosters mutual respect and understanding.

USING POWER WITH CHILDREN

Using power with children involves fostering open communication and collaboration. This means having conversations with children to explain the reasoning behind rules and boundaries, allowing them to understand and participate in decision-making processes. Empowering children to have a say in decisions that affect them, such as activities or food choices, helps build their confidence and self-esteem.

It's also important to listen to their feelings and validate them, even if we don't always agree. Collaborating with children to find solutions to problems strengthens their problem-solving skills and helps them feel valued and heard. While we ultimately have the final say, the emphasis should be on teaching and empowering our children to grow into independent and responsible adults within a supportive and nurturing environment.

Real authority in parenting doesn't mean that we simply have control over our children. It involves collaborative efforts with our children to equip them with problem-solving skills and the ability to make responsible decisions. Once we have established our authority in the boundaries stage, we should begin to take on the roles of teachers, guides, and protectors, creating an environment where our children can thrive, learn, and grow into responsible and independent individuals.

As you read these descriptions, you likely found that you can relate to both on some level. There are so many factors that influence our parenting that we don't often fit neatly into any box. However, as with impulse and impact parenting, you likely related to one of these descriptions more than the other. If you relate more to power with, you will probably agree with most of what you read in this book and will find insights into using the relationship you've built as your kids transition into young adults. If you relate more to power over, then don't worry—you are not alone! I tended toward, and still do from time to time, power over parenting. I have gradually learned to move away from this, and I am excited to share that with you!

We are all in this together and we can all learn from each other!

SELF-REFLECTION

Consider your current power dynamics in your parent-child relationship. Do you feel that you have more power over your child's decisions and actions, or are you working collaboratively with your child to empower them? Are there specific areas in which you'd like to shift from power over to power with?

....

....

....

....

....

....

....

FINAL THOUGHTS

The foundations in this chapter are fundamental to Impact Parenting. Throughout this curriculum, you will find that everything you learn will be rooted in or expand upon one of them.

While you will find a few strategies in this book, you will find mostly principles. Families are different, and even the same Snapshot can play out in many different ways depending on the family makeup and dynamic. I find principles to be more universal, so I teach principles that parents can apply in the best way(s) for their families.

For example, holding boundaries is a principle. Redirecting is a strategy that you can use to hold a boundary. Not every child will respond to redirecting, but every parent can hold a boundary. Another example is family time. Creating family time is a principle. Eating dinner together is a strategy that helps us create family time. Not every family can eat dinner together, but every family can find time for family time.

The principles you find in this book will act as guideposts, helping you find your way through the journey of parenthood. As you weave these principles into your daily parenting routine, you'll find that they can be adapted to fit your unique family style, bringing harmony and balance to your parenting.

↓ THINK AND DISCUSS

Considering the topics we have covered in this chapter, reflect on the following Snapshots. If you are in a group setting, take some time to discuss them with each other. Remember that there isn't always a single right or wrong answer. There are many considerations and perspectives to explore, so embrace the opportunity to engage in meaningful conversations that broaden your understanding and encourage critical thinking.

IN THIS CHAPTER, WE DISCUSSED:

- Impulse vs. Impact
- Reacting vs. Responding
- The Stages of Parenting
- The FACT Check
- Power Over vs. Power With

SNAPSHOT 1
BROKEN LAMP

Six-year-old Sam accidentally breaks a vase while running through the house. He has been told multiple times not to run in the house.

→ **Jason's Response**

Jason tells Sam that he is irresponsible for running in the house when he knows better. He sends Sam to his room. Later, Jason allows Sam out of his room, but there was no discussion about what happened.

→ **Adam's Response**

Adam grabs a broom and dustpan and enlists Sam's help with cleaning up the mess. While cleaning, Adam asks Sam what he learned from breaking the lamp. They discuss actions and consequences. And they come up with a plan to help Sam remember not to run in the house.

→ **QUESTIONS TO CONSIDER**

1. What stage of parenting does this Snapshot reflect, and why is that important?

2. Explain the difference between the two approaches. How might each one affect Sam?

3. How might you handle this within your family?

SNAPSHOT 2
THE MOVIES

Fifteen-year-old April is allowed to meet her friends for a movie and walk to a restaurant right next door by themselves for the first time.

→ **Charlotte's Response**

"I'm so excited for you! I know you understand about respectful behavior. Is there anything you're not sure about? Remember, you can always text or call me if you feel nervous or uncomfortable. Do you remember how to tip at the restaurant?"

→ **Priscilla's Response**

"Don't be rude to anyone. And don't be too loud in the theater. Don't be on your phones or talking during the movie. That's rude. And don't be one of those bratty kids at the restaurant that is rude to the waiter. If you can't handle this, you won't be able to do it again."

→ **QUESTIONS TO CONSIDER**

1. What stage of parenting does this Snapshot reflect, and why is that important?

2. Considering what you know about power over and power with, explain the difference between the two approaches. How might each one affect April?

3. What message might each response send to April?

4. How might you handle this within your family?

2

THE BOUNDARIES STAGE

Ages 1 to 5

THE BOUNDARIES STAGE

Boundaries make our children feel safe, allowing them to fearlessly explore their worlds.

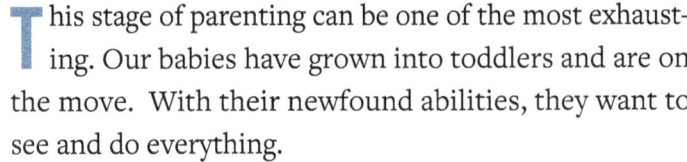

This stage of parenting can be one of the most exhausting. Our babies have grown into toddlers and are on the move. With their newfound abilities, they want to see and do everything.

Setting and holding boundaries is difficult for many parents and can be one of the most frustrating seasons for parents. It is time-consuming and thankless—we set boundaries and our kids repeatedly try to push the limits. (It doesn't help that the boundaries stage happens during what might be the cutest season of our children's lives!)

Our job is to outlast our kids and hold firm with our boundaries until they understand!

While demanding, the boundaries stage is also incredibly important. Healthy boundaries create a healthy foundation for the parent-child relationship. Unlike friendships, where there should be a balance of power and authority, parents are the authority over their children—boundaries help establish this authority.

Boundaries also make our children feel safe, allowing them to fearlessly explore the world. Knowing that their parents will be there to stop them before they go too far allows kids to move confidently through their world. Unfortunately, they don't make the connection yet between boundaries and their safety. That's why they push back. They also push back because they were created to explore. Consistency and routine help them explore, find boundaries and understand that those boundaries are firm.

COMMUNICATION IN THE BOUNDARIES STAGE

Children at this age are like sponges. They soak up the sights, sounds, and conversations around them. When we take the time to answer their questions and engage in conversations about their world, we are also helping them strengthen their communication skills. The more conversations our children have, the stronger their communication skills become.

Conversations during the boundaries stage usually aren't deep. Instead, they are more about figuring out the rules and understanding how things work. While this may seem trivial to us, this type of learning is important to our young children. When they ask us questions, even those that seem silly, it is important that we treat their questions with respect and take an active part in the conversation.

Our willingness to have conversations with our children also shows them they are important to us. If we brush them off or show frustration, it can communicate that their questions are a burden, and this may discourage them from asking questions in the future.

Imagination is important. Be open to their crazy ideas—dream with them and get into their world. Let's not be so wrapped up in our responsibilities that we forget how to imagine with our children!

Our Words Matter

Our words can build our children up or tear them down. Most of us have or have had some belief about ourselves, whether positive or negative, that came from the words our parents spoke over us. If our parents focused mainly on correcting our wrongs and changing our less-than-desirable character traits, we probably grew up with negative beliefs about ourselves. If our parents focused on praising our victories and cultivating our positive character traits, we probably grew up with positive beliefs about ourselves. Of course, most of us have a mix of beliefs about ourselves based on our many life experiences, but our parents or primary caretakers most likely had a major influence.

Psychologists have found strong evidence that our beliefs and expectations impact the outcomes in our lives. This phenomenon is known as the self-fulfilling prophecy. The basic idea is that if we believe something, then we subconsciously bring it to fruition.

One of the most famous studies about the idea of the self-fulfilling prophecy was conducted in the 1960s.[1] Teachers had the wrong information about their students' intelligence and abilities. Later findings showed that these struggling students, whom the teachers had believed to have higher intelligence and ability, actually improved a lot.

How does this apply to parenting? Our words will impact our children. Whether we intend to or not, we influence our children with our words. What we say and how we say it matters.

We've heard many of them before. Speak to the behavior, not your child's character, don't criticize them, etc. These are basic principles that we should all be working on, but there are also other, less obvious ways that we communicate with our children.

Look at these examples of how the self-fulfilling prophecy can play out in the home.

When our child treats us rudely or disrespectfully, we tell them that they are rude or disrespectful. The more it happens, the more we let them know that

---

1   Rosenthal, R., Jacobson, L. "Pygmalion in the classroom". Urban Rev 3, 16–20 (1968). https://doi.org/10.1007/BF02322211

they are rude and we don't appreciate it. As we begin calling them out more, they start acting more rude and the cycle continues.

Whenever our child messes up, we tell her that we are disappointed. When she stays up too late or fails a test, or forgets to write thank you letters for a gift, we say, "I'm so disappointed in you." Over the years, she starts to believe that she is a disappointment and will never make us happy, so she quits trying.

Whenever we don't want our child to do something, we tell them something bad will happen. If they climb on things, they will fall. If they wander away, they will get kidnapped. If they don't study, they will fail and have to repeat a grade. If they drive to the next city they will get into a car wreck. Eventually, our teen becomes fearful. Rather than trying new things, our teen avoids new experiences for fear of what bad things may happen.

SELF-REFLECTION

Consider the message you are sending with your words. What unintentional messages are you sending? Are they more positive or negative? What kind of messages do you want to send with your words? How can you make one tiny change in the way you communicate with your children?

....

....

....

....

....

....

....

CONNECTION IN THE BOUNDARIES STAGE

There is no magic shortcut when it comes to setting and holding boundaries.

The boundaries stage is often the most physical of all the stages. Our kids want to see and touch us, and we may find it difficult to get a moment alone without leaving the house altogether! For some of us, constant contact is wonderful. We love all the snuggles and hugs and snotty kisses. For others, we need some downtime. Neither is right or wrong. We are simply created differently, just like our children.

However we feel about our toddlers' incessant need to touch us, it is important that we return their touch. We don't have to be their living blankies, but we can attempt to snuggle, hug, and be close to them. Like communication, physical connection in the boundaries stage is more about quantity, but we can still set some boundaries.

As our children continue to grow and mature, the dynamics of our connections will naturally evolve, and our interactions will gradually shift from a focus on sheer quantity to a greater emphasis on quality time spent together. As they become more independent and develop their personalities, we can foster deeper connections by engaging in meaningful activities, heartfelt conversations, and shared experiences. While the physicality of the boundaries stage may ebb and flow, the bond we forge with our children through touch and connection will continue to evolve and strengthen.

DISCIPLINE IN THE BOUNDARIES STAGE

It's no secret that children want to rule their world (and us)! Our job is to teach them boundaries and help them understand that we are in charge. I wish there was a magic shortcut, but there just isn't.

HOLDING BOUNDARIES

Often, we set boundaries, our kids push the boundaries, and we cave. Let's face it: they are younger and have more energy and fewer responsibilities. They have nothing to do all day but try to get past our boundaries!

So how do we hold boundaries?

It is pretty simple—we do not give in. When we set a boundary, we stick with it. If we decide our toddler must ride in the cart at the grocery store, then that is a boundary. Holding the boundary means that no matter what the child does, they must ride in the cart, even if we have to leave the store and try again another time.

Sometimes this results in walking through the grocery store with a red-faced, crying, screaming toddler. But if we can survive a few times of this, then our kids will get the picture—there is nothing they can do to get their way.

Holding boundaries is a way to teach our children where the boundaries are and to establish our authority. When we create a boundary as the authority figure, we demonstrate to our children that the boundary will not move just because they test it. If there is a consequence, our child knows it ahead of time. If there is no consequence, we consistently guide our child away from the boundary.

Holding boundaries is not a one-and-done process. It will take some time for our children to understand. The amount of time depends on our consistency and how strong-willed our children are. Consistency is key.

If we can consistently establish and hold boundaries, we can parent from a foundation of authority and focus on building relationships while parenting for impact. Otherwise, we are likely to spend the rest of our parenting years fighting for authority.

How comfortable are you with setting and maintaining boundaries? How has this been reflected in your parenting journey? Consider those times when you don't hold them. What generally leads to your giving in?

....

....

....

....

....

....

....

PBS MODEL FOR DISCIPLINE

How we communicate through discipline matters. When we correct, we should keep it simple. Instead of overwhelming them with lengthy explanations or convoluted instructions, it's best to keep it simple and concise. By using clear and straightforward language, we help our kids understand the specific behavior that needs correction and the consequences that follow.

Polite | Behavior Focused | Simple

The PBS model helps us to remember this in those tense moments before we lose our cool. At this stage, kids just need to know what they can and can't do. Focusing on behavior helps us correct our children rather than criticize them.

We also have to remember to be intentional in avoiding reactions. When we see our kids doing something wrong, we can sometimes feel like it's a reflection on us, which can stir a reaction. Remember to pause for a moment in order to find a response and avoid a reaction.

For example, when we see our child throwing rocks at birds, we might wonder how they could do such a mean thing to an animal. In reacting to that thought, we might yell at them, "You're so mean! Stop throwing rocks!" However, when we take a pause, it gives us a chance to shift to a PBS response such as, "Remember, we do not throw rocks. They can hit someone and hurt them."

If we walk into the kitchen to find our toddler coloring on the table, we can find our anger spiking pretty quickly. After all, the table could be ruined. We might react with something like, "Why would you do this? You've ruined the table!" But, as with most emotional reactions, this will most likely confuse the child. While they know they have upset us, they may not completely understand why. A PBS response might look more like this, "I see you did some coloring, but it would have been better to do it on paper. Can you do that from now on? Let's get this cleaned up."

As with most reactions, those in the examples above come from a place of anger or frustration. When responding out of frustration, we will most likely lean toward a critical reaction. When we react emotionally, we are really teaching our kids to read and navigate our emotions. When we take a moment to pause, we can shift to responding rather than reacting. Our PBS responses help our children understand the consequences of their actions and empower them to make better choices in the future.

CONSEQUENCES VS. PUNISHMENT

Consequences are meant to teach, while punishment is meant to shame or embarrass a child and force them into submission. While punishment may appear effective in the moment, it often results in worsening long-term behavior. As children test boundaries, logical consequences can teach them where boundaries are in a healthy and productive way.

USING CONSEQUENCES EFFECTIVELY

Be Calm

Anger and other elevated emotions have no place in discipline. When we punish out of our emotions, we are teaching our children to navigate our emotions rather than how to control their own behaviors. Giving discipline when we are angry creates an inconsistent and fear-based environment. As much as possible, stay calm and make the behavior your focus.

Be Clear

Clearly define boundaries and any consequences your kids will face if they cross them. Surprise punishments only serve to create a fear-based submission to rules. Remember, when kids know the boundaries and consequences ahead of time, they can feel confident exploring the world around them.

Be Consistent

Defining boundaries is one thing. You must also teach your child that the boundaries are firm, or they will constantly test them. This requires a consistent response. When our children cross a clearly defined boundary, they should get the same result each time.

Be Quick

When a child makes a bad choice, they need to understand it immediately. Implementing a consequence later in the day will not be effective because they can no longer connect the consequence to the action. Similarly, taking away an event or activity happening later in the week won't have the effect of an immediate consequence that is connected to the action.

Be Connected

Consequences are meant to teach—make sure the consequence is connected to the action, and always explain the behavior and the consequence. Logical consequences are a great way to teach children about the effects of their actions. For example, when a child takes her shoes off in the car, then she will have to ride in the shopping cart or stroller rather than walk. When logical consequences are not available, make the consequence fit the action as much as possible.

When we react emotionally, we are teaching our kids to read and navigate our emotions.

Be Fair

Fair consequences are age-appropriate and fit the behavior. Missing out on a trip to the park because they threw their food on the floor doesn't fit the behavior. Having to miss a birthday party doesn't really fit the behavior of taking their shoes off in the car. This is too much for a toddler to understand.

Be Adaptable

Sometimes kids get used to the same consequences and become immune to the effects. Be ready to switch gears when necessary, but also make sure to give your plan time to work (a week or two usually gives you a good idea). If the consequences aren't working, try something else!

ASKED AND ANSWERED

When our kids start begging, pleading, arguing, reasoning, or using tactics to get their way, we can use these three words: Asked and Answered. Like magic, they can shut down the begging. When our child asks to go to the park and we say no, they might beg: "Please, please, Mom, PLEAAAAAAASE!" We can simply say, "Asked and answered."

For this to be effective, we must stop talking—don't say another word on the subject! It will take a few times for them to realize that we are serious (longer if we have caved to their behavior in the past), but stick with it. Once they realize it's not working, the begging and pleading should stop.

SELF-REFLECTION

How can you create a balance between setting boundaries and fostering a loving, supportive relationship with your child?

....

....

....

....

....

....

....

MODELING APPROPRIATE BEHAVIOR

Our children learn from observing the world around them, especially the behaviors of their parents and other significant adults in their lives. They watch how we talk, how we act, and how we treat others. They use these observations to develop their own behavior patterns. So we must be mindful of the messages we are sending through our words and actions.

We often do this well in the beginning. We model language and behavior for our babies and toddlers. It's a fun, monkey-see-monkey-do situation. They see us and we see them immediately try to copy what we are saying or doing. As they get older, they quit following behind us, mimicking our every move. It's easy to forget that they are still watching us.

My daughter was about two and had been going to daycare for a few months. One day when I picked her up, the teacher told me a funny story. She said that a new friend had started that day and was sad about it. The girl had been crying for a good bit when my daughter put her hand up (talk to the hand style) and said, "She is crying for no reason!"

WOW. The teacher thought it was funny, and it was. But it was also like having a mirror held up to myself, and honestly, I didn't like what I saw. I realized I had to be intentional with my words. My kids were soaking up everything. They weren't just learning the lessons I taught them; they were learning the lessons I modeled as well.

If we know and accept the fact that modeling is impactful, then we can use it powerfully. Aside from limiting our negative words and behaviors, we can be intentional in modeling positive behaviors. We can model the positive behaviors that we want to see in our kids. We can use our words to build them up, encourage them, comfort them, and give them a feeling of security and safety in our homes. We can give them an example to follow as we model the healthy choices we want them to make.

Remember, modeling appropriate behavior does not mean that we have to be perfect. We will make mistakes because we are human. Our mistakes show our kids that we are human and provide us with an opportunity to model characteristics such as humility, grace, authenticity, and integrity.

People learn by watching others, and our kids are no different. If we want them to behave a certain way, then we must step up and model the behavior for them. We are the most influential example in our children's lives, and we are teaching them whether we realize it or not. It is important that we reflect on exactly what we are teaching them.

SELF-REFLECTION

Have you ever seen your child do something and realized that they looked just like you? How did it make you feel when you realized the impact of your modeling on their behavior? What steps can you take to be intentional in modeling positive behaviors for your children, and how can you navigate the moments when you make mistakes in front of them?

....

....

....

....

....

....

....

FINAL THOUGHTS

The boundaries stage is a physically demanding one. For some of us, myself included, it is the most difficult stage we will experience. It is so much of the same thing over and over. We might feel like we are constantly repeating ourselves (we are) with no result, but the fact is that we are laying a foundation. We are establishing our authority and setting the parameters of our relationship with our children.

Boundaries should be established by the time our children are five years old. Boundaries are the foundation of a healthy parent-child relationship. Our children must know that while we love them and will support them, we are the authority in the relationship. When we establish our authority early, it can pave the way for a smoother transition into the teen years.

As our children go through adolescence and all the changes that come with it, it can be a comfort for them to know the dynamics in the household. Knowing that they are not in charge, while frustrating, can be comforting because it also means that they are not responsible. Boundaries are more than just a way to keep our kids in line. Healthy boundaries are integral to healthy development for our teens.

If we didn't establish firm boundaries before the age of five, that's okay. It can be done when they are older. It may take more time and effort because our kids have become used to having some sort of control, but we can still establish a healthy parent-child dynamic. If this is the case for you, it is important that you take some time to do this as soon as possible. It will make a positive difference throughout the teen years. In Chapter Six, titled "Family Reset," we will explore the process of re-establishing our authority and developing healthy family relationships.

↓ THINK AND DISCUSS

Considering the topics we have covered in this chapter, reflect on the following Snapshots. If you are in a group setting, take some time to discuss them with each other. Remember that there is not always a single right or wrong answer. There are many considerations and perspectives to explore, so embrace the opportunity to engage in meaningful conversations that broaden your understanding and encourage critical thinking.

IN THIS CHAPTER, WE DISCUSSED

- Communication: Our Words Matter
- Holding Boundaries
- PBS Model
- Using Consequences Effectively

SNAPSHOT 1
WALL ART

Three-year-old Asher is pitching a fit because his dad will not let him color on the wall. After telling Asher twice not to color on the wall, Asher does it anyway. His dad takes the crayons away, explaining that he cannot use them to color on the wall. Now Asher is crying and yelling, "No!" at his dad.

→ Jason's Response

Jason sits down with Asher and says, "I know you are upset. I'll sit with you until you feel better." A little while later, Jason says, "I know it was hard to lose your crayons, but remember, you cannot color on the walls."

→ Adam's Response

"It's hard to like you when you act like that. Go to your room until you can calm down! This is nothing to cry about." Adam walks away.

→ QUESTIONS TO CONSIDER

1. What underlying message do you think Asher might take away from each response?

2. Consider what we have learned in Chapter 1 about reacting and responding. How does that apply here?

3. How might the Pause and the FACT Check help parents in this situation?

4. What could be some long-term effects of each type of response?

SNAPSHOT 2
SPELLING WORDS

Five-year-old Layla wants to watch her favorite cartoon, but her mom tells her she must finish writing her spelling words first. Layla tells her mom that she finished them in class. Her mom checks Layla's folder and finds the work incomplete.

→ Charlotte's Response

"Layla, you lied to me! How could you? Lying is terrible, and when you lie, no one will trust you! How can I trust you now that you have lied? Go to your room and finish your homework!" Later, when Charlotte calms down, she says, "I know you wanted to watch your show, but lying is wrong, and I won't be able to trust you if you lie to me."

→ Priscilla's Response

"Layla, you told me that you finished your work, but I have it here and it's not finished. Let's sit down and talk about this." With the TV off, Priscilla asks, "Why did you think you needed to lie to me?" After Layla's explanation, she says, "I understand why you did it, but lying is not okay. Go ahead and finish your homework and no more TV today. We'll try again tomorrow."

→ QUESTIONS TO CONSIDER

1. How is Priscilla's response different from Charlotte's response?

2. Considering Layla's age and the stage of parenting, is the depth of Priscilla's response appropriate?

3. What do you think would be the most effective response with your own child(ren) at this age?

3

THE TEACHING STAGE

Ages 6 to 12

THE TEACHING STAGE

The relationship we build with our children now will greatly affect our experience with them as teenagers.

While the boundaries stage is about setting and holding boundaries and establishing our authority, the teaching stage is about going deeper with our kids. During this stage, our toddlers turn into big kids and then tweens. Our parenting begins to shift from more physical–tugging at and clinging to us–to a more mental state–explanations and conversations. This is the time when we begin training the heart and building influence with our children.

The teaching stage is the time for cultivating a strong relationship with our children. The struggle here is that they seem to be testing our patience at every turn. We can feel like we are constantly correcting them, and most likely, we are. It is how we do it that will make a huge difference in our relationship with them. And it is important to understand that the relationship we build with our children in the teaching stage will greatly affect our experience with them as teenagers.

As we train our children and try to raise them in the way they should go, the Bible tells us that they will not depart from it when they are older.[1] In the midst of our kids making mistakes and testing boundaries, it can be easy to forget the "when they are older" part. Let's remember to give them room and give ourselves some grace during this stage. Stay the course and see what God does!

1   https://biblehub.com/niv/proverbs/22.htm

COMMUNICATION IN THE TEACHING STAGE

Around the age of five, kids begin to wonder why things are the way they are. They ask questions (many, many, MANY questions) about things we have never even considered. One of my favorites was the time my five-year-old daughter asked, "Who lives with nobody?" (That question actually sparked a great conversation!) While answering so many questions can be tiring, let's keep in mind that God created kids to be curious, planting in them a genuine wonder for the world that He created. In His infinite wisdom, He also created a season of parenting that inherently lends itself to deepening our connection with our kids.

During this stage of parenting, we begin to shift to a more relational connection with our kids, and it's important that we recognize the need for this shift early. It is during this stage that we lay the groundwork for the influence we will need in the next stage of parenting. When our kids transition into the teen years, they will decide whether or not to remain under our authority as they push boundaries and seek freedom from our rules.

Kids ask a million questions! Let's try our best to answer them all! Our children are naturally curious. When we engage with them in their curiosity, we can foster a love of learning. Rather than answering their questions directly, we can point them in the right direction and encourage them to think critically about potential answers or provide them with age-appropriate resources to help them explore.

The relationship we build with our children today will be the basis for the influence we have with them during those pivotal years, and we have to begin building that relationship earlier than many of us realize. During this stage, our children are genuinely interested in what we have to say and are eager to learn from us. We have an opportunity to be their first and most influential teachers. It's our chance to share values, knowledge, and wisdom that will shape their understanding of the world.

TEACHABLE MOMENTS

Teachable moments are examples from a child's experiences that can be used to teach valuable life lessons. This is not about proving our kids right or wrong. The goal of a teachable moment is to highlight something our child might not see and help them understand it and how it might fit into their life.

Our daughter came home one day and told us all about a fight that happened in school. She told us that one kid's collar bone was broken and he was sent to the hospital. We asked her if she had seen this happen herself, and she said that her friend told her. We talked about how stories can get twisted as they pass from one person to the next. The next day she came home and told us that she saw the boy at school. His collarbone was not broken and he had not been taken to the hospital. Now, when she tells us something that is a rumor, we relate back to this event and remind her of the possibility that it could be completely untrue and encourage her not to pass along information that she isn't certain to be true.

TEACHABLE TIMES

Teachable times are any time you think your child will be open to learning and listening to you. Most teachable moments happen naturally, but you can also create them. Sometimes they may ask a question or experience something that opens a door to a conversation and serves as the backdrop for a teachable moment.

Never use a teachable moment during a crisis or time when your child's emotions are elevated—they simply won't be able to process or learn. Circle back when your child is calm (12-48 hours after the event is a good time to revisit and have a conversation).

USING TEACHABLE MOMENTS

Be on the lookout for opportunities to work teachable moments into your daily life. They can appear when we least expect it. For example, if we get a speeding ticket, we can talk to our kids about obeying the law. A trip to the grocery store can become a lesson in budgeting. Even a simple walk in the park can be a chance to discuss nature and the environment. These moments often provide the setting for valuable lessons.

Be ready to abandon the moment.

For teachable moments to be successful, we need to be receptive to our kids' moods and selective about the moments we choose. Again, during a crisis or a difficult situation is never the time to teach a lesson. Be sure the mood is relaxed before trying to make a moment teachable.

Set aside your expectations.

Sometimes when we try to teach our children something, we want them to get our point right then. We want them to understand the lesson and agree with the message. Teachable moments, however, are more about planting seeds in their minds and hearts that they will harvest when the time is right. We might drop a giant wisdom bomb in front of our kids and get nothing more than a blank stare and a shoulder shrug— that's okay. They might disagree with us, completely confident that we are wrong. That's fine, too.

Make it relatable.

Be careful not to turn teachable moments into lectures. Usually, a brief sentence or two can sum up whatever we are trying to say. We should make our point quickly and move on. Our kids will ask questions if they want to.

Not every moment has to be teachable.

The more we use teachable moments, the more perceptive to opportunities we become. It can be tempting to take every opportunity to teach our kids valuable lessons, but it's important not to create a culture of constant teaching. Our kids also need opportunities to experience and process life themselves.

SELF-REFLECTION

Have you been mindful of creating teachable moments for your children based on their experiences and questions? Can you think of any recent situations where you successfully turned an everyday moment into a valuable life lesson for your kids? Consider whether you've been too zealous about creating teachable moments for your child. How can you slow down to notice something he or she is teaching you?

....

....

....

....

....

....

....

HOW TO BE A SAFE SPACE

Sometimes we unknowingly create a sense of distrust for our kids when it comes to sharing their most vulnerable thoughts, feelings, and fears. Becoming a safe space for them to share is incredibly important for building trust and influence with them. It takes time and effort to become a safe space, but the payoff is well worth it.

Treat their problems with respect.

When our kids bring their minor problems to us, we need to treat them with respect rather than diminish or minimize them. Kids relate to the world differently than we do, and something that may seem insignificant to us can be a big deal for them. We don't have to oversell our empathy, but we also shouldn't brush them off or belittle their feelings. How we treat their small problems tells our kids how we will treat their big problems.

Be open and authentic.

When we open up to our kids about our struggles, it shows them we are approachable. Our authenticity and openness will show our kids that we can relate to them. If we have struggled with something similar, then sharing it with them appropriately can show them we can empathize with them. However, we need to be careful that we are not sharing a similar struggle just to minimize their feelings or to make it about us.

How we treat their small problems tells our kids how we will treat their big problems.

Listen without judgment.

When we judge our kids or even make judgmental comments, then we are setting ourselves up as an unsafe space for their deep needs. When they open up to us about something, no matter how small, we can listen without judgment. This will be difficult to fake, so we need to work on sincerely trying not to judge our kids. It can be hard because they can definitely do and say some head-scratching things. But the goal is to show them we are a safe space where they can share their struggles, failures, and concerns without fear. (Sometimes it is important to focus more on the long-term goal of becoming a safe space than the short-term goal of winning an argument.)

Listen without lecturing.

Often, when our kids bring a problem to us, it results from a mistake that they've made. When we immediately begin lecturing them about what they did to bring the problem on themselves, we become unsafe. That doesn't mean we can't have a conversation about what went wrong. It just means that the time to do it is not when they open up to us. When our kids reach out to us and open up, the best thing we can do is listen, be curious, and be empathetic. Ask questions and let your kids talk. We can always circle back around for another conversation where we talk about behaviors and consequences.

Control your emotions.

When our kids come to us with a big problem, we may find ourselves emotionally elevated. If we can remember to pause, then we can take a deep breath and respond instead of reacting. Emotional reactions will only push our kids away. When they come to us with a problem, they are looking for support, wisdom, and strength. When we react emotionally, we are showing that we may not be equipped to help them with their problem. It is important for us to remain a solid, stable source for them as they navigate their teen years.

SELF-REFLECTION

What are some strategies you use to become a safe space for your children to share their thoughts, feelings, and fears? Are there any instances where you can recall building trust through your approach to listening and understanding your children?

....

....

....

....

....

....

....

CONNECTION IN THE TEACHING STAGE

As our kids move out of the boundaries stage and into the teaching stage, most of them will become less physical. During this time, we should begin creating more relational connections with our children. We can do this through conversations, shared activities, trips, and outings together. Though they are getting older, connection with our children will still come naturally during this stage. They still see us as fun and want to hang out with us; not to mention, they don't really have a choice since they have no money and can't drive.

While time together happens naturally, the teaching stage is a great time to start having some more intentional time together as a family. While this "family time" may happen naturally during these years, it can become more difficult as our children grow up and spend more time outside of the family circle. Intentional family time is a great way to continue to connect with our maturing children.

FAMILY TIME

Family time is a great way to connect and build strong relationships with our kids. It can look different depending on your family, but the principle remains the same: to cultivate and maintain family connections. Like the Sabbath, family time is for our good, so as our families grow and our kids mature, it should shift to meet the needs and dynamics of our family. Consistency is key—it's more important we make time to connect rather than get caught up in worrying how we connect.

Like gardening, we won't always see the immediate results of our efforts. But don't give up! We are parenting for the future, planting and cultivating before the harvest. Keep this in mind, especially during the moments when family time fails to meet expectations. Sometimes family time will be forced and not everyone will be overjoyed to participate (ahem, teenagers!), but we still need to be consistent and make it happen. We'll be glad we did.

MAKING THE MOST OF FAMILY TIME

Start early.

The earlier we start, the more natural it will be for our kids to gather and connect as a family. It's easier to create

Like gardening, we won't always see the immediate results of our efforts. But don't give up!

this habit when they are younger and more naturally inclined to spend time with us but remember that it still may take time to get used to. A conversation can help pave the way for starting intentional family time.

Start small.

Start small with a 5-10 minute conversation about everyone's day or week—doing this a couple of times a week can serve as a quick win and help build the foundation for longer, more robust time together. Starting with hour(s)-long family time could feel forced, create conflict, and make you feel like giving up entirely.

Building family time into activities you are already doing is a great tactic. Dinner time or car rides to school are natural times to intentionally connect. You're already together; you just need to shift the conversation. Find what works for your family and make it happen!

Start with a conversation.

We can start by talking to our kids about what we are trying to do with family time. We might even take suggestions from them about what might work for our family. They often have great ideas, and giving them a voice also helps them take ownership of the process and feel a sense of responsibility for its success.

Be consistent.

Like with most aspects of parenting, consistency is key. Whether that's once a week or once a month, whatever we decide to do for family time should be something we can maintain. Starting with what we can do consistently sets us up for success—we can always take it up a notch later.

Be flexible.

It's important we give new things a fair shot, but if it's not working, we can pivot and try something new. (To be clear, a fair shot is more like five to ten times of trying, not two or three.) If we don't give ideas time before scrapping them, we can find ourselves in a cycle where nothing seems to work.

Another way to be flexible is to tweak something when it doesn't work rather than scrapping it altogether. If you plan for your family time to be Saturday morning, but you find that one or more of your family always seems to be gone, then maybe try Sunday lunch or dinner.

Keep it light.

This can be difficult for rule-followers and those of us who need order, but keeping it light is important to the success of family time. Remember the whole purpose is to connect and strengthen relationships within the family rather than to participate in a power struggle about behavior, attention, or respect. Start light and create your family time habit before taking conversations to a more serious level.

Yes, we can force it.

Not everyone will be excited about family time, but it's okay to remind your family that it's important and that you're doing it regardless. But we have to set the tone, and our kids should follow our lead once they realize we aren't caving to their expectations. It's much easier said than done, but we need to make family time happen and keep a positive attitude. The strong family relationships will be well worth the effort.

One time, we were given tickets to a college football game. My husband and I decided that it would be a great family day. We told the girls about it and got the same response from both of them: "Do we have to go?" I responded, "Yes." When they began to moan and groan, I said, "We are going and so are you. That is not going to change. We understand that you don't want to go, but you have a choice to make. You can make the best of it or you can make the worst of it. That's up to you."

Our kids chose to make the best of it, and we had a great time. It is difficult sometimes because when we think of family time, we want to think it will be filled with fun and heartfelt moments. When we force our kids to participate, we are afraid they will make it miserable for everyone or we will be stuck attending to their happiness. By placing the responsibility for their enjoyment on them, we can free ourselves to have fun (and it's often contagious!).

SELF-REFLECTION

How consistent are you in having intentional family time with your kids? What are some challenges you face in maintaining this consistency, and how might you overcome them? Do you expect too much of yourself and your family when it comes to maintaining family time? How can you create a balance between intentionality and flexibility?

....

....

....

....

....

....

....

DISCIPLINE IN THE TEACHING STAGE

As our kids continue to grow and develop, we should adapt our approach to correction and discipline as well. Rather than giving them directives, begin shifting to conversations. This shift not only empowers them to think critically and make decisions but also allows us to listen to them and understand their perspective. Through open dialogue, we can guide them in making informed choices while still maintaining our authority.

This transition is a natural and healthy part of parenting. Just as our connection with our children evolves from physical to relational, our discipline evolves from the PBS model to a more collaborative one.

3-C APPROACH TO DISCIPLINE

The goal of discipline is not to punish our kids for their mistakes, but to guide them as they learn to manage themselves.

The 3-C approach to correcting our kids provides an outline for discipline that teaches and encourages growth. The goal of discipline is not to punish our kids for their mistakes, but to guide them as they learn to manage themselves. This principle gives us a model that will help us do that. We can adapt it to meet the needs of our homes. Regardless of the situation, the model and the principle remain the same.

Curiosity

When we enter a situation with curiosity rather than accusations, it makes our kids feel safe and gives them room to explain their thought process. It creates space for conversation and even collaboration on a solution, which can help strengthen the relationship. Our approach doesn't mean there won't be consequences, rather it sets the tone for a more collaborative encounter as opposed to an argumentative one.

Conversation

A conversation is more than a judgment or decision that we hand down. It is a two-way process in which we give our kids room to share their thoughts, opinions, motivations, feelings, etc. Our job is to guide them—sometimes they need some wisdom, sometimes they need education, and sometimes they need understanding and grace.

Correction

How we correct our kids makes all the difference. It might seem counterintuitive, but giving them a chance to self-correct can go a long way in strengthening the parent-child connection. They may need guidance even after trying to self-correct, and we can help them figure out the best path if necessary. Or we may need to implement new boundaries. It's our job as parents to make these decisions.

One dad, Anthony, stored cash in his dresser drawer for emergencies. He found his son, Jackson, taking money from the drawer. His first thought was that his son was stealing from him. Rather than accusing him, though, Anthony asked genuinely, "Why are you taking money from my drawer?" Jackson told him that he needed it to buy souvenirs on his upcoming field trip.

Furthering the conversation, Anthony asked his son why he didn't just come to him for the money. Jackson told his dad that he seemed so busy with his work project that Jackson didn't want to bother him. Jackson also explained that he knew his dad would say yes to the money, so he thought he would just get it himself. Anthony explained the importance of respecting his private space and asked for an apology. Jackson agreed and promised not to do it again.

Because Anthony started with curiosity, rather than accusation, they were able to talk about the problem rather than argue. Jackson didn't completely understand that he was doing something wrong and once he did, he said he would not do it again.

SELF-REFLECTION

Think about a recent situation where you needed to correct or discipline your child. Did you approach with curiosity or accusations and directives? Reflect on how your approach affected the outcome and your relationship with your child. How could the 3-C approach enhance your relationship with your children? How can you balance maintaining your authority while also empowering your child to make informed choices?

....

....

....

....

....

....

....

FINAL THOUGHTS

The teaching stage is a transition between childhood and adolescence, and it is an important time for us to build upon the foundation of authority with relationships. As we see the toddler years slip away, we'll begin to see glimpses of the young adults they will become. While the questions can add up and become overwhelming at times, this stage can bring a lot of joy and wonder as our kids explore their world.

During this stage, our relationship with our children begins to deepen, and we should develop intentional times of connection that will set the stage for the incredible journey of coaching and guiding our children into adulthood. As we guide our children toward independence, we can hold onto their childlike qualities for a bit longer. Take some time to enjoy this season.

↓ THINK AND DISCUSS

Considering the topics we have covered in this chapter, reflect on the following Snapshots. If you are in a group setting, take some time to discuss them with each other. Remember that there is not always a single right or wrong answer. There are many considerations and perspectives to explore, so embrace the opportunity to engage in meaningful conversations that broaden your understanding and encourage critical thinking.

IN THIS CHAPTER, WE DISCUSSED

- Teachable Moments
- Being a Safe Space
- Family Time
- 3C Approach to Discipline

SNAPSHOT 1
SIXTH GRADE DANCE

Arya's middle school (grades 6-8) holds dances for students. Arya's parents set a boundary that their kids would not attend dances in sixth grade. With the first dance approaching, Arya excitedly recalls her experience of a boy who asked her to the dance and her telling him that she could not go. When her mom, Charlotte, asked her how she felt about that, Arya responded, "Actually I was kind of glad that I wasn't allowed to go. I didn't really want to go with him, and I don't know if I could have said no because I didn't want to hurt his feelings."

→ **QUESTIONS TO CONSIDER**

1. What lesson about life can be highlighted here?

2. How could Charlotte use this moment to reinforce their (the parents) role as guides and protectors?

3. Consider your natural reaction to this situation in light of what we have learned in this chapter.

4. Would you naturally consider this a teachable moment?

SNAPSHOT 2
BURN BOOK

The second-grade teacher calls Tanesha's parents and tells them that Tanesha has made a list of unkind things about another student (Mae). The teacher also informs them that she believes Tanesha was coerced to do it by another student (Sonya). She also confides that Sonya often pits Tanesha and Mae against each other.

→ Adam and Priscilla's Response

When Tanesha gets off the bus, both parents are there to meet her. Adam starts, "How could you do something so mean? I raised you better than that!" Then Priscilla, "I am ashamed that you could be so cruel to someone! You are grounded for two weeks! No phone. No TV. No friends! Go to your room!"

Dinner that evening is very tense because everyone is still feeling emotional from the afternoon. Tanesha is afraid to get her parents started again, so she says very little. There is little conversation and once dinner is over, Tanesha goes back to her room for the rest of the evening.

→ Priscilla's Response

When Tanesha gets off the bus, both parents are there to meet her. Jason tells her that they spoke to the teacher and know what happened, but they want to hear from her also. He says, "Take some time to think about everything and sort it out in your head. We'll talk after dinner. I want you to know that we love you no matter what, even when you make mistakes—big or small."

Dinner is pretty normal. While they all know that there is a difficult conversation coming, they are able to enjoy dinner and talk about their days. Tanesha is not fearful of her parents' reactions, so she talks openly about her day.

After dinner, they sit down to talk. Tanesha explains what happened from her perspective. Jason says, "I think a personal apology to Mae is in order. What do you think?" Tanesha agrees. Charlotte says, "It sounds like Sonya is not really acting like a friend. I also think that you should take some time away from Sonya. Over the next couple of weeks, I would like you to find two new friends to play with." Tanesha agrees and they talk through the details of what the apology and making new friends will look like.

QUESTIONS TO CONSIDER

1. Explain the difference between the two approaches. How might each one affect Tanesha?

2. What could be a benefit of allowing Tanesha some time to think before discussing her actions?

3. If Adam and Priscilla had used the FACT Check, what might they have discovered?

4. Can you recognize the 3C approach in Jason and Charlotte's response?

5. How do power over and power with apply in these situations?

4

THE COACHING STAGE

Ages 12 to 18

THE COACHING STAGE

They may seem self-sufficient, but they still need us—just in a different way.

The teenage years. If you know, you know. If you don't, you will. I cannot tell you how many parents have come to me in complete shock. Even though we talked about it ahead of time. They read this chapter, and we talked about what would happen. And they were still shocked when they watched their kids morph right before their eyes. Moms whose snuggly young boys that adored them, suddenly found themselves being iced out. Shooed away. Parents found themselves face to face with a teen who seemed to completely dismiss all logic and reasoning.

The attitude, the impulsivity, the emotional roller coaster, the personality changes. It can be a lot for us parents. And it can be tempting to detach from them and, honestly, hide until it passes. After all, they seem self-sufficient. It can feel safer to just let them be until some sort of sanity returns. But I want to encourage you to hang in there. I want to give you some insight into what is actually happening and encourage you to resist the urge to leave your teens to it. They may seem self-sufficient, but they still need us—just in a different way. As you read on, my prayer is that you will begin to feel more equipped to support your teens as they make the journey to adulthood.

THE TEEN BRAIN

Children's brains experience a massive growth spurt when they're very young. By the time they're six, their brains are nearly 90-95% of adult size.[1] These early years are a critical time for brain development, but the brain still needs a lot of remodeling before it can function as an adult brain.

PREFRONTAL CORTEX

→ LOGIC

AMYGDALA

→ EMOTIONS

The prefrontal cortex is the front part of the brain and is responsible for logic and decision-making. The amygdala is located at the back of the brain and is responsible for our emotions. The remodeling process begins in the back of the brain and works toward the front. Because the prefrontal cortex is the last to develop, most teens rely on the amygdala to make decisions. This is where their impulsive actions and overly emotional responses originate.

---

1   https://raisingchildren.net.au/pre-teens/development/understanding-your-pre-teen/brain-development-teens

Our family was cleaning up after dinner one evening when my twelve-year-old daughter grabbed a glass of water. She stood with her back to the sink and with no warning, she threw the water from the cup over her head. It landed all over the sink, the counter, the floor, and the window. I was dumbfounded, but knowing enough to PAUSE, I took a breath. Then I said, "You are not in trouble, but I need to know why you did that." Just as surprised as all of us, she said, "I just wanted to see what would happen!"

Another time, my fourteen-year-old daughter came upstairs and showed me a blue ink stain on my new throw blanket. I asked her how it got there and she said, "I was bending the pen because I wanted to see how far it would bend without breaking. Then it broke." Again, I paused. I asked her what she learned from this, and she said, "I shouldn't bend pens." I asked her if she would do that again, and she told me she would not.

These are two examples of youthful impulsivity at its best, of acting without thinking. I hear so many of these stories from frazzled moms, many of whom wonder what is wrong with their children. Most of the time, nothing is wrong—they are just teens with developing brains and little access to their prefrontal cortex.

EMOTIONAL EFFECTS

As teenage brains develop, their emotions are taking a roller coaster ride, and their responses are often out of proportion. They can't find their favorite red shirt and it's suddenly the end of the world. Or they make a poor grade on an assignment and profess they will fail out of

While these responses can seem over the top, they feel real to the teens who experience them.

school. Maybe they strike out and blame themselves for losing a game and consider quitting the team. While these responses can seem over the top, they feel real to the teens who experience them.

It's important to remember that their stress is real. They face school and social stresses along with the everyday stress of meeting expectations placed on them. All of this while they are often managing their time between sports, activities, and schoolwork.

As our teens go through major transitions, we'll see resistance, a change in attitude, mood swings, and other behaviors that seem out of character. This can be tough to watch as a parent, but remember it's normal. It's our job as parents to lead by example, showing our teens how to self-regulate their emotions.

While they need fewer rules and boundaries, they still need some. They will push against them, but they want them. This can be a confusing time for teens and parents.

As parents of teens, we should shift our role from teacher to coach, stepping back to allow our children to make decisions. Teens will not listen to us in the same way they did before. We can no longer be directive. The way we teach them is by holding boundaries, modeling appropriate behavior, and being supportive.

Take the role of the coach: give advice but allow your child to make the ultimate decision, suffering the consequences of poor decisions and reaping the rewards of good ones.

WHAT DOES THIS LOOK LIKE AS A PARENT?

During the coaching stage, our kids are practicing for real life. As their parents, we need to give them the chance to make decisions and face the consequences of their choices, which means backing off the rules. We need to let them run the plays, but be ready to call a timeout to make necessary adjustments.

SELF-REFLECTION

Considering what we learned about the teen brain, did you have any "Aha!" moments in this chapter? Can you relate to situations where your teenager(s) exhibited impulsive behavior or emotional responses that seemed out of proportion? How did you handle these moments? Looking back, what might you have done differently to support them effectively?

....

....

....

....

....

....

....

DISCIPLINE IN THE COACHING STAGE

Knowing when and how to step back and shift into the role of coach, advisor, and supporter can be tricky. Here are some ways we can transition into the coaching stage.

Do it gradually.

Don't let go of everything all at once. Be strategic and give your teen control over an area where you think they will be successful—it will help them gain confidence. Often these are areas where our kids have proven their maturity.

Do it willingly.

Sometimes we struggle with giving up control and we begrudgingly give it to our kids, making them feel bad or incapable in the process. Remember, this is a natural part of maturing, and we shouldn't make our teens feel guilty or ashamed about their desire for autonomy. Jesus was twelve when he left his parents and headed to the synagogue on his own.

Move to real-world consequences.

Part of giving up control and letting teens take the reins is letting them learn to make judgments on a smaller scale and experience the consequences, which should no longer be mainly parent-determined.

As your teen makes decisions, your input should be real-world-focused as much as possible rather than self-focused or based on a parent-determined consequence. As adults, we have to weigh the consequences of our actions, and this is a great time to help our teens learn this skill by scaling back our imposed consequences and accepting risky decisions that may or may not work out for them.

Let go of unnecessary rules.

Once we train the heart, the rules aren't as important. As our kids learn to make decisions for themselves, they don't need as many directives, and we should begin letting go of some of the rules. Letting them figure things out on their own will also have a bigger impact than if we tell them how to do everything.

This can be a complicated process for parents. While we must ensure our teens are safe and healthy, providing too many rules can stifle them. Remember, they will naturally begin to seek independence. In this stage, we can help our teens learn to make responsible decisions by holding boundaries while also providing them with freedom and flexibility.

Think about some of your current rules, especially the ones your children complain about the most. Are these rules still necessary? When you are considering a rule and deciding whether or not to keep it, ask yourself these questions:

What is the purpose?

Who is the rule *really* for?

Is the rule still necessary?

STRATEGIC FREEDOMS

Strategic freedoms refer to age-appropriate opportunities for teens to make choices and take risks within safe and reasonable boundaries (like choosing activities or socializing with friends within certain time frames). As our teens begin to navigate their way through adolescence and strive toward independence, giving them strategic freedoms can help them develop a sense of responsibility and autonomy while allowing us to maintain a level of authority and guidance. Giving teens the chance to practice decision-making skills in a controlled environment helps prepare them for adulthood while still ensuring their safety and well-being.

KNOWING WHEN TO STEP IN

Sometimes our kids will find themselves in over their heads. It is tough as a parent, but we have to decide when to let our kids struggle and figure it out themselves and when to step in and stop them, advocate for them, or take action on their behalf.

Knowing when to step in can be difficult. As parents, we often feel our kids' pain as much as they do. Of course, we want to fix it or make it go away, but if we intervene too much or at the wrong times, we are only hurting them more in the long run. Life experience teaches us so much more than words.

> "Prepare your child for the path rather than preparing the path for your child."
>
> – Tim Elmore

This is a great place to start when considering whether you should step in and take matters into your own hands. Most of the time, we can help our kids more by walking them through their difficult times rather than solving their problems or making them disappear. When we step in to solve our children's problems, we are communicating that they are not capable of doing it themselves.

My daughter was sick a good bit during the first semester of school. At one point she missed an entire week of school. She was trying to talk to her teachers and get help catching up with the instruction she missed. After school each day, I asked her how it was going. She told me that her teachers seemed to be blowing her off. They didn't seem to want to help her catch up.

This was her perspective, and I had not spoken to her teachers. Rather than step in and ask for the work myself or demand that her teachers help her, I sent an email. I explained that she had been struggling with an illness that had caused her to miss more days than normal. I explained that she was working hard to get caught up and we were helping as much as we could. I asked them to let me know if there were any areas where she was not meeting expectations.

Teachers get all sorts of excuses, and it is hard sometimes to know when kids are exaggerating or actually being truthful. When I realized that my daughter's voice was not being heard, I simply lent her mine then stepped back and let her take it from there. Once the teachers realized that my daughter was truly struggling and working to get back on track, they began helping her more. She was able to catch up and it worked out.

So how do we know?

It can be difficult to know when and how to step in for our teens. Sometimes they seem to be on top of things and sometimes they seem to be ready to fall apart. Here are some questions to ask yourself that can help you determine whether or not you should step in.

Will this have a long-term impact on my child's future?

Sometimes we feel like something will have a long-term impact when it really won't. Failing to study for a ninth-grade math test? Not so much. Going out with friends who you know use drugs? Maybe so! We should consider the long-term consequences before we step in. If they are minimal, then it might be best to allow our teens to handle the situation and see where it leads. We can always step in if necessary.

Is this impacting my child's overall health or well-being?

As teens, lots of things will impact them emotionally, and they can tend to overreact to normal situations. Keep in mind that they can tend to unload on us, and then immediately feel better about a problem. If you are concerned, keep an eye on the situation and look for signs of emotional, physical, or mental distress. You can also have your child evaluated by a mental health professional if you feel that something is really wrong.

Is this too big for my child to handle?

Be sure you understand your child's capabilities, which are usually much more than we give them credit for. Often, we tend to see our kids differently depending on our relationship with them. For example, teachers see kids as students, capable of learning, growing, and rising to the challenges set before them. This view helps teachers allow students the space to struggle on their own. As parents, we can often see our kids as our babies that need to be nurtured and protected, and we struggle to allow them to struggle, even if it's what is best for them at times. When we view our children as unable to handle challenges, we might frequently step in to shield them from the struggle. In turn, our children will internalize this belief in their own incapability, perpetuating a self-fulfilling cycle.

Does my child want my help?

Sometimes, we can feel the need to jump in and help our kids handle their problems, but as they get older, they may want to start handling things on their own. That's a good thing. Our job is to ask in a calm, nonjudgmental way so that they might feel comfortable admitting whether or not they need help—they usually know when they need it and when they don't.

Has my child proven that they are not ready or cannot handle this?

Sometimes we give our children freedom, and they show us that they are not ready yet. If so, then we need to step in and rework the boundary. Be sure to do this compassionately. There doesn't always have to be a consequence or a lecture. A simple, "Hey we tried, and it didn't work, let's try again in a month." will do.

Have you considered the idea of strategic freedoms for your teenagers? Are there areas in which you might gradually grant them more control to help them develop confidence and autonomy?

....

....

....

....

....

....

....

POWER STRUGGLES

Power struggles have gotten a bad reputation and are often seen as a sign of disrespect, but they are a part of growing up. They are inevitable as our kids seek independence and push against our boundaries. There are actually two types of power struggles, and one of them is a natural part of the transition to adulthood.

Resistant vs. Defiant

A resistant power struggle is when a teen questions and pushes against boundaries in a healthy way, simply looking to have more control over the choices they make. We have to determine where control needs to be given and where it doesn't. Most of the time, teens don't agree with our decisions, so we often find ourselves in resistant power struggles.

Defiant power struggles are when a teen outright defies boundaries and uses unhealthy tactics to get their way. When teens are confronted with a boundary that they don't like, they may argue, yell, call names, repeatedly question, or use other tactics to wear their parents down. A tween or teen will use many tactics to get us into a defiant power struggle if they feel they can get their way.

AVOID DEFIANT POWER STRUGGLES

If we are in a resistant power struggle, then we should be able to sit down and have a discussion with our child. If our child refuses to hear what we are saying and persists in having his or her way, then we are likely in a defiant power struggle. If you find yourself in a defiant power struggle, then you have likely lost. Why? Because your child has proven that they can challenge you and draw you into an argument. If we give in to power struggles when they are young, then we are setting ourselves up for more and bigger struggles as they get older.

If you have begun implementing the principles we have talked about earlier, then you will hopefully find that the defiant power struggles are few and far between. Stepping back, reducing the rules, and allowing our teens some autonomy will greatly reduce their need to fight every rule they don't like. Transparency, authenticity, and a deep connection will help them trust our motives and also reduce the defiant power struggles.

Understanding that power struggles will happen, we can also make an effort to limit the frequency. We can take measures to ensure that when they do arise, they are more

When we give our kids the tools to do something the right way, then we are setting them up for success.

resistant than defiant. Here are some ways to navigate power struggles and keep them from becoming defiant in nature.

Don't make it about us.

Remember that we are shifting from parent-determined consequences to real-world consequences. We should be sure to communicate this with our children. Rather than say that we don't want them to have Snapchat because we don't like the secrecy, we can make it about the risks involved. Another example is communicating that curfew is to keep them safe and remove unnecessary temptations rather than because we don't trust them or don't like them being out that late. If we cannot think of a real world consequence, then we may need to reevaluate the rule or boundary.

Teach them the right way to challenge authority.

When we give our kids the tools to do something the right way, then we are setting them up for success. Oftentimes, our kids go about things the wrong way because they haven't been taught the right way. When they challenge us in an inappropriate way, then we might consider whether or not we have taught them how to challenge us in an appropriate way. When we teach them how and offer them an avenue for challenging rules, then we often find that they don't really desire to defy us, they just want to have their case heard.

Allow them to challenge appropriately.

Sometimes, a resistant struggle can escalate to a defiant struggle because we are not willing to hear our children out. If they do challenge a rule or decision, then we should be open to discussion, as long as they are being polite and appropriate. We should be sure that we truly listen to them and are open to their suggestions. We might find that they make some valid points and some changes can be made.

Identify your child's objectives.

When our children challenge us, even in a defiant way, we can seek to gain an understanding about why they are upset about the rule. We can try to see their objective in challenging it. We might even ask them to explain their position. When we find out their motive, we may be able to come to an agreement that works for both parties.

Take a pause.

When we sense a power struggle coming, we can stop the conversation and take a minute to gather our thoughts. We can take time to consider our own perspective and our child's perspective. We might change our mind or we might not, but we can restart the conversation on our own terms.

Offer choices.

Remember that our tweens and teens are looking for autonomy and freedom. They are not quite ready to take adulthood head on, so choices are a good way to give them control in smaller doses. We can do this by avoiding rigidity in our rules and allowing them to negotiate a bit. If we ask them to put the dishes away and they ask if they can do it after they finish their show, then sure. If there is a reason they can't, such as we need to start dinner, then we can say no and share that reason.

Refuse to participate.

Once a decision has been made, then we can simply refuse to participate in any further discussion. Sometimes we hear our children out and they don't like that we didn't change our minds, so they start to argue. At this point, we can simply say, "I heard you and I made the decision and I am no longer going to talk about this." Then we can walk away. The key here is to refuse to talk about it anymore.

SELF-REFLECTION

Have you experienced power struggles with your teenager, and if so, can you distinguish between resistant and defiant power struggles in your interactions? Reflect on your own personal view of your children challenging your authority. How open are you to listening to their perspective and considering potential changes, provided they express themselves politely and appropriately? What specific situations come to mind where your teenager challenged your boundaries, and what were their underlying motives or needs in those instances?

....

....

....

....

....

....

....

CONNECTING IN THE COACHING STAGE

When my first daughter was a baby, people would tell me that she was going to hate me when she was a teenager. As a new mom, I wasn't sure what they meant, but I knew that I was not going to just accept this as a fact without trying to prevent it from happening. Today, I understand what they mean. The teenage years are tumultuous! Thankfully, I did not accept the words spoken to me so long ago. I worked to build a healthy relationship with my children. Now that they are teenagers, we struggle sometimes, but our relationships are strong.

Our developing teens can have attitudes for days, but we don't have to accept that they will hate us. Just because they begin to seek independence doesn't mean that we have to pull away from them—we can keep cultivating the relationship. We just need to know that it will look different from when they were toddlers.

The amount of time we spend with our teens will likely decrease, so our intentionality needs to increase—we need to make the time we have with our teens count. We should invite our teens to spend time with us, and we need to keep inviting them even when they turn us down.

This is a time that can easily get away from us. Our kids are not constantly asking for our attention and may even be a bit averse to spending time with us. The lure of our own bed, the sofa, the tub, the book, or whatever that thing is that we never got to do for the last twelve years is strong. But we must find a balance.

For some of us, it will be hard to let go, and we may find ourselves creating too much intentional time. For others, it may be easy to slip into this new life of doing our own thing, and we may find ourselves neglecting to spend any time with our teens. During this new season, it's important to find a new normal and a healthy balance as a family. As teens get older they will want more time to themselves. That's okay—time spent together becomes more about quality over quantity.

Even as our teens seek independence, we can continue to cultivate the relationship.

Remember the family time we covered in the teaching stage? Now is the time it becomes really valuable. As our teens drift away from us, family time can be a great way to maintain a healthy connection with them. Trying to maintain a routine that we have been doing for years is difficult, but doable. When our teens are used to intentional time together with family, then we will likely receive less pushback from them as we continue it. It will probably look different and become less frequent, but we can still keep it going.

CHANGES TO HOW WE CONNECT

As kids get older and we're no longer treated like a human jungle gym, the physical effort of parenting is reduced. However, the mental effort involved in parenting a teen can be exhausting and overwhelming. Teens need more emotional connection and support, but they will also need more independence. One minute they are snuggling up to you, asking you questions, holding a meaningful conversation, and the next they are rolling their eyes and telling you that you're out of touch with reality!

Connect on their terms.

As our teens mature, they will begin to pull away from us, no longer willing to spend long periods of time with us. The things we did to draw them in when they were younger will no longer hold their interest, so we should observe their interests and find new ways to connect with them.

We can invite them to spend time with us in different ways, some of which will work and some won't. When they decline, simply move on without making a big deal about it. Let them have some freedom to choose when and how they connect with us—when we remove the pressure, the invitation becomes more appealing.

Settle for less.

Our teens need to identify who they are without us, which means that they need to shut us out. As scary as it is, it is part of their natural development process. We need to be comfortable settling for less of their time and attention. We may get less of their time, but this leaves us with more energy to make the most of the time we get—remember it's quality over quantity!

Neither of my daughters enjoys shopping or going out to lunch, both things I dreamed of doing with them when they got old enough. I have one who loves to play games and one who loves to read and watch TV. So, I have become a fan of Yahtzee and teen dramas.

Both of my daughters have active social lives, and it is not uncommon for my husband and I to find ourselves with a kid-free weekend. We use these times to do the things we enjoy individually and with each other. When our kids have plans without us, we just don't make a big deal out of it, even if it seems like they are choosing their friends over us.

Instead, we continue offering to spend time with them and remain available when they need or want to spend time with us. We also have regular family times together that help us ensure we are connecting with our kids throughout this season.

Embrace a quiet connection.

Connection is not always about conversation, shared activities, and teachable moments. As parents, we may find ourselves desperately trying to fill empty air space with words of wisdom or encouragement. But just being present with our kids is as important as teaching and connecting with them. We need to get comfortable with silence. When we are sitting in silence with our teens and feel the urge to fill the space with a conversation, we can remind ourselves that this is a cozy connection time, and it is also important.

Time With vs. Time Near

Time near our children is valuable and creates connection. Spending time together quietly doing our own thing can strengthen the bond we have with our kids, creating an easy, laid-back feeling within the relationship. This is important because we spend so much time shaping and molding our kids that it can be tiresome for us and them.

Spending time near our children is important, but we also need to remain intentional about spending time with our children, engaging them in conversation and shared activities. This intentional interaction plays a vital role in nurturing strong parent-child bonds and fostering a healthy relationship.

SELF-REFLECTION

Think about the evolving nature of your connection with your child. How has your relationship changed as they've grown and sought more independence? Consider your child's interests. What are some ways you can connect over things they enjoy?

....

....

....

....

....

....

....

COMMUNICATING IN THE COACHING STAGE

The way we communicate with our teens continues to change in the coaching stage. Teens will not listen to us in the same way they did before, and we can no longer expect them to hang on to our every word. We teach them by holding boundaries and supporting them. Conversations should be more open and based on mutual opinions. (Be ready to be questioned and challenged!)

CHANGES IN HOW WE COMMUNICATE

While these changes may seem overwhelming or even a little scary, there are things we can do to shift our communication from the directives that we used with our little ones to a more open style that allows room for our teens' thoughts and ideas.

Stay honest and authentic.

I cannot express enough how important it is for us to be authentic and transparent with our kids. They know us and know when we struggle. So it makes sense to let them in on it. They often understand much more than we give them credit for. But when they lack the details, they fill them in from their own limited bank of experiences. As parents, if we can be open and honest about our lives and our parenting journey, we can create a deeper connection with our kids.

Ask questions.

Our kids have a lot to share, and how we listen makes a big difference. We need to step up our listening game and shift how we respond to their ideas. When they make a statement, we need to respond with a follow-up question rather than our opinion. When they say something that we don't agree with, rather than share our opposing view, we can ask them to share more about how they came up with the concept.

Let it go.

Our kids are going to challenge our beliefs, whether out of frustration or because they sincerely believe we are wrong. They may even do it just for the sake of challenging us. Sometimes their ideas will be valid and come from a thoughtful place. Sometimes they will come from a place of misunderstanding or a lack of experience. We don't have to correct everything they believe right now. Life will teach them a lot, so we should be wise about when and why we take a stance.

Stop and think.

We can easily become defensive, especially when we feel challenged by our children. The crazy thing is, they may just have a point. Rather than take an immediate defensive posture, stop and ask yourself if they have a point. If they do, be willing to acknowledge and talk about it.

Be respectful.

Our kids are young adults, and we need to respect their experience in the world, however limited it may be. We should be courteous and respectful in conversation with our teens. If this is new for you, start by talking to your teen the way you would an adult that you respect. How would you respond if you disagreed with them? We are not giving our teens the freedom of an adult, just the respect and consideration. This will go a long way when they are choosing whether or not to remain under our authority.

SELF-REFLECTION

Consider where your child is now in the coaching (or any) stage of parenting. Does the communication style match the stage?

....

....

....

....

....

....

....

START WITH A CONVERSATION

When We Change

We've all been there. We read a book, listen to a podcast, or join a small group and suddenly we are full of ideas that will surely get our kids under control. We design our reward systems, glitter our chore charts, and rhinestone our kindness jars. We get going and can't wait to see the change in our kids. Then we realize about a week or two in that we can't keep up. So we give up, leaving the charts to sag on the wall and the jar to get lost behind the stack of mail on the counter.

Looking back, I can identify those times when my own mother was trying some new strategy to get us to listen and behave. As a kid, I thought she was crazy because I had no idea what she was doing. I had no clue that she wasn't sure how to parent us. When we try out new strategies, especially when we keep quitting and trying new ones, our kids probably think the same about us.

But we are not the only ones growing and changing. Our kids are developing their own moral system, cultural outlook, style, and personality. They are trying new ideas and letting go of old habits, maturing in many ways while they stay the same in others. As God's creation in a fallen world, we are all a work in progress.[1]

Before we make big changes in our home or in our parenting, why not let our kids in on the plan with a conversation?

A simple, honest conversation can help us avoid a lot of confusion as we try new things with our children. When we communicate with them about our plans, we are more likely to be consistent in carrying them out, and where we are not, at least they know we are not crazy! Consistency

> Before we make big changes, it is important to talk to our kids about it.

---

1 Ephesians 4:22-24

also creates a feeling of safety for our children. When our kids know what to expect, they can relax and focus on growing and maturing.

When They Change

Instead of jumping to conclusions about our kids, let's start with a conversation. When we see something that is concerning or when our kids appear to be veering off course, we can talk to them about it. Rather than making assumptions, we can approach them with curiosity and initiate a conversation. Remember, approaching with curiosity will help us start conversations on a neutral or positive note.

Remember that a conversation is a two-way street. As much as we share and talk about our concerns, we should listen to our children share their thoughts as well. We also need to respect their thoughts and opinions. The more we model open conversation, the more receptive our children will be to talking openly with us.

Remember that our kids are not always going to be ready to talk when we are. My twelve-year-old daughter does not enjoy serious conversations and is often resistant to them. We respect this about her and do not force her to talk. When she does open up, we try to avoid pressing her for more. We let her determine how much she wants to share.

Sometimes we need her to talk to us about an issue or share with us about a situation. Maybe something happened at school and we need to hear details from her or we might be worried about her because of a certain experience. In these instances, we tell her ahead of time that we need to have a conversation. We let her know what we will need from her, maybe some information or some sharing of feelings, and then we give her time to process and prepare. She will generally open up and give us what we need. Sometimes just barely, but that's okay.

We can't force our kids to talk to us. We can try, and it may work for a while, but forcing conversations will only cause damage in the long run. Our job is to create a safe space so that our children feel comfortable coming to us.

SELF-REFLECTION

Consider the concept of creating a safe space for your teen to come to you for discussions. How do you currently approach this in your family? Is it difficult for you to allow your child or teen the freedom to decline conversation? Reflect on the balance between fostering open communication and allowing your teen the time and space they need.

....

....

....

....

....

....

....

FAMILY CONVERSATIONS

Family conversations are a great way to guide and equip our kids. These conversations can be intentional or they can be organic. We might find our family together in a room and conversation starts flowing. This is a great time to go with the flow and see where it goes. While organic conversations are important, it is also good to make time for intentional conversations with our families.

When we make conversations a regular part of our daily lives, it creates a sense of unity and deepens the connections within the family. These conversations are also a way to equip our kids and prepare them for the world they will encounter.

Creating intentional family conversations can be a challenge, especially if our family is not used to getting together regularly. But, if we can overcome the challenges, the reward can be great! These tips can help your family start your own routine.

Create a space.

Sometimes creating a specific time and place for deeper conversations can help our kids be more open to sharing. Consider a time when everyone is likely to be home. This might be easier with younger kids because we are their social planners. If you have older kids, it may take some time to get everyone together. Remain consistent and don't give up. Once the routine is created it will become more natural.

Start small.

If your family is not used to having intentional conversations, then start small and build from there. Keep it light at first and gradually build up to the deeper topics. You might start with a quick talk about the new plan. Spend 5 minutes telling everyone about it and ask them back next time. Starting small leaves room to build up to a more substantial connection time.

Set some guidelines.

Setting some ground rules for conversations can keep them positive and productive. We can do this intentionally with formal rules that we lay out ahead of time, or we can do this by modeling appropriate conversation etiquette and addressing issues as they arise. Either way, be sure to allow some time for everyone to get used to the format.

Remember the goal.

The goal of family time and conversations is to equip our kids and create a safe space. We do this by planting seeds and sharing our thoughts in a nonjudgmental way. Don't get hung up on the success of each individual experience. It will be the sum of our whole efforts that will count.

Don't force them to talk.

While we can make our kids attend family time, we can't make them participate. If one or all of your kids are not feeling a talk at a certain time, then let it go. Spend the time just sitting quietly or talking with the rest of the family. If we try to force them to talk to us, then we will likely end up in a power struggle and damage the goal of creating a safe space. We can always pick back up at the next family time.

SELF-REFLECTION

Are there specific challenges you face in maintaining regular family conversations? If so, what are they, and how do you plan to overcome them?

....

....

....

....

....

....

....

FINAL THOUGHTS

The coaching stage can be one of the most difficult stages for some of us. Our children are changing right before our eyes and we are often caught off guard by them. It can be a chaotic stage with so much growth and development happening so quickly. When we enter this stage prepared for the changes, then we can better support our kids as they develop.

These years bring a change in the parent-child relationship. The power begins to shift from us, the parents, to our children. They begin to challenge our rules and authority. They begin to break away from their childhood attributes and try on new, more adult attitudes and behaviors. They even begin to break away from us. These things can seem daunting for us as parents, but understanding the developmental process that is behind all the changes can help us shift our mindset from a rule-based approach to a more conversation-based one.

THINK AND DISCUSS

Considering the topics we have covered in this chapter, reflect on the following Snapshots. If you are in a group setting, take some time to discuss them with each other. Remember that there is not always a single right or wrong answer. There are many considerations and perspectives to explore, so embrace the opportunity to engage in meaningful conversations that broaden your understanding and encourage critical thinking.

IN THIS CHAPTER, WE DISCUSSED

- **Teen Brain Development**
- **Strategic Freedoms**
- **Power Struggles**
- **Changes to How We Connect**

Remember that each child and each family is different. There is no fundamentally right or wrong answer. We want to apply the principles in the best way within our own families.

SNAPSHOT 1
THE TV SHOW

Bree has been watching a TV show that her parents have told her not to watch. When Jason catches her watching it and tells her to turn it off, she refuses and declares that her parents never let her do anything and are treating her like a baby. Jason says that's not true, but Bree yells at him, "Yes it is!" When Jason responds, Bree interrupts him, telling him that all of her friends are allowed to watch the show and demands to know why she can't. Jason explains that he needs to talk with her mom about it first, but Bree continues to interrupt him, saying that they are so unfair.

→ **QUESTIONS TO CONSIDER**

1. Is this a resistant or defiant power struggle and how could Jason handle it?

2. Should the parent consider giving Bree a strategic freedom at this point?

3. How can Jason create a safe space in this moment? What are some common reactions that would create an unsafe space?

SNAPSHOT 2
TENNIS CHALLENGE

Alexis is a seventh-grade tennis player on the middle school tennis team. After the first few practices, she tells her dad, Adam, that her coach keeps putting her on a court with players who are well beneath her level. She also tells her dad that she heard that her coach only plays the eighth-grade players in matches. Alexis feels discouraged because she knows that she can outplay several of the eighth-grade players. She also knows that most teams allow players to move up seeds, or ranks, by challenging those above them.

→ **QUESTIONS TO CONSIDER**

1. How do Alexis' age and the stage of parenting come into play?

2. Should Adam step in or allow Alexis to handle the situation?

3. What are some ways that Adam could coach Alexis through this situation?

SNAPSHOT 3
HOME ALONE

Adam and Priscilla do not allow their children to be at a friend's house when there are no parents home. The rule has been in place since they were young. Now Rama is 14 and has asked to hang out at her best friend's house after school and do homework. Her friend's parents won't be home from work, so they will be home alone for a couple of hours. Priscilla says no because no parents will be there. Rama explains that she is allowed to stay home alone now and asks her mom to reconsider.

→ QUESTIONS TO CONSIDER

1. This example reflects a resistant power struggle. Consider some healthy and unhealthy responses for Priscilla.

2. Should Priscilla reconsider the rule in this situation?

3. What role do strategic freedoms play in the Snapshot?

5

PARENTING AND TRAUMA

PARENTING AND TRAUMA

Trust in us helps our children feel secure as they navigate their world.

Trust is the foundation of the parent-child relationship. Trust allows us to build a deeper connection with our kids and creates a safe space for open communication and honest dialogue—where our children can be vulnerable and express themselves fully. Trust helps our children feel secure as they navigate their world. When a child experiences trauma, it can erode their sense of trust in adults, authority, their friends, and even us. When trust is missing, our children can feel unsafe and anxious in their own worlds.

Trauma does not always have to be a big event. For our children, it can be anything that shakes their foundation of safety. In preschool, a teacher read *The Teacher from the Black Lagoon* to my daughter's class. It is about a substitute teacher who turns out to be a monster and burns students up with fire from her mouth. The book was really scary for my daughter. She felt scared and alone and we were not there to protect her. This is not a huge deal to her now, but at the time it was traumatic. Her experience caused some struggles through elementary school that she needed help working through.

TRUST AND PARENTING

God can restore flesh from dry bones and stone hearts.

Trust can be broken in ways both big and small. Sometimes trust is broken gradually over many small events that chip away at a child's confidence. Sometimes a big moment shatters a child's security. However trust has been broken, repairing it is important.

TRUST ERODED IN SMALL WAYS

When we break trust in small ways over time, it can slowly chip away at our children's confidence in us and gradually break down the relationship. This can happen over time through many small events, like broken promises, hurtful interactions, inconsistency in parenting, or even minor deceptions. These seemingly small incidents can build up over time and cause our children to withdraw from us emotionally as they get older.

As we learn new principles, we will likely begin to recognize those times when we are breaking our kids' trust in small ways. When we do, it is important that we begin to acknowledge our actions and take responsibility for them. If you feel that you have broken your child's trust in small ways over time, it's important to begin rebuilding that trust. Remember that a great way to begin anything new with our kids is by having an honest conversation.

The Power of Apology

As we move forward with these new parenting principles, we are going to mess up and get it wrong. The important thing is that we make it right. Just as we have our kids apologize when they have made a mistake and hurt someone, we need to do the same with them.

Many of us fear that apologizing to our kids will make us appear weak or that we will lose our power. Apologizing actually makes us look safe. It may not feel important when our children are younger but as teens they will be looking to unload their fears, worries, big decisions, and mistakes. And they are going to be looking for a safe place to do that.

To them, a safe place is someone who understands, listens without judgment, and empathizes. While we need to tell them the truth and not just what they want to hear, we can do it with empathy. And when we get it wrong, we can apologize.

Apologies should have a single focus and a single message: our behavior and our responsibility.

Our apologies should focus on our actions, not our children's behavior. When we apologize, we should make it clear that we are responsible for our actions. We should place no expectations on our children for how they respond to our apology. If they respond inappropriately, we should address it later rather than during our apology.

I have had a lot of practice apologizing to my kids over the years. One day, I walked into the living room and saw that it was a mess, I snapped at my daughter. I told her to get the mess cleaned up, and I was tired of them always leaving their things lying around.

As I said it, I could see my daughter's demeanor change—she was hurt. Honestly, my outburst was not about her. The house is frequently messy because we live in it, and when it gets out of control, we clean it. But that day I was frustrated by something unrelated and took it out on her.

After she straightened up, she went to her room. I went up there and said to her, "I apologize for snapping at you. You didn't do anything wrong. I was frustrated and took it out on you. I'm sorry." She looked at me, eased herself into her closet, and closed the door. At that moment, I wanted to tell her that she was being rude, but I didn't. I

Apologies should have a single focus and a single message: our behavior and our responsibility.

"And I will give you a new heart, and a new spirit I will put within you. And I will remove the heart of stone from your flesh and give you a heart of flesh."

(Ezekiel 36:26)

As we model apologizing and forgiveness, we are modeling humility and grace for our children.

walked away. Had I addressed her behavior, the apology would have been forgotten.

Let's remember that as parents, we're not perfect. We are bound to mess up and make mistakes along the way. The important thing is how we handle those moments and make them right. Sometimes, that means swallowing our pride and apologizing. While apologizing to our kids might seem unnatural for us, it is actually one of our most powerful tools as parents. It demonstrates humility and teaches them the value of accountability and forgiveness. It shows them that we're not perfect, but we're willing to acknowledge our missteps and make amends.

Our genuine apologies become powerful life lessons, shaping their understanding of empathy, communication, and healthy relationships. So, let's embrace the courage to apologize when needed and help foster an environment of understanding and growth within our family.

Modeling Forgiveness

Modeling God's grace and forgiveness for our children is an incredible opportunity. We may find this easy to do with our infants and toddlers, but as our kids grow up, they will mess up on larger and larger scales. The larger their mistakes, the more frustrated we can get.

It's when we are frustrated that our responses matter most. Of course, we are annoyed that our kids have destroyed or lost something valuable. We can get angry and punish them in an attempt to teach them a lesson, or we can choose to forgive them.

Offering forgiveness in moments of frustration or anger isn't easy. It takes self-control to respond rather than react, but if we can pause and take a breath before speaking, the results can be incredibly beneficial for our children.

We can say, "I know it was an accident. I forgive you." When we do this, forgiving our children in the midst of their worst mistakes, we are modeling Christ's love in a powerful way.

Sometimes we mess up, too. After we apologize to our kids, we also need to ask for forgiveness. This can be incredibly difficult because we are giving them some power and that can be scary. However, forgiving is something that God calls us to do. It also benefits the forgiver more than the offender. Our mistakes can provide an opportunity for our children to practice forgiveness and experience the power of forgiving.

As we model apologizing, asking for forgiveness, and graciously forgiving others, we are building a firm foundation of humility and grace for ourselves and our children.

SELF-REFLECTION

Take a minute to reflect on yourself and the trust you have with your children. Give an honest assessment of where you believe you stand with them. Celebrate the positives and commit to working toward healing and rebuilding any areas of broken trust.

....

....

....

....

....

....

....

TRUST SHATTERED IN BIG WAYS

When a child experiences broken trust in a profound way, such as abandonment, dangerous living conditions, or death of a loved one, especially over a prolonged time, the process of rebuilding is more involved. While our children readily forgive us for those small missteps, forgiveness may not come as quickly for a child who has been through trauma due to our prolonged actions. As we talked about earlier, children who have been through trauma are not always in control of their emotions and may need help processing their experiences before they can consider forgiving and trusting again.

This process is just that, a process. It is meant to provide a guideline and is certainly not the only way to rebuild trust with children. These steps are meant to be helpful for parents as they navigate rebuilding trust with their children.

Put yourself in your child's shoes and see things from their perspective.

Try to put yourself in your child's shoes and grasp the mix of emotions they're going through—a blend of love and hurt. Remember that their perspective may be different from yours, so it's important to respect their unique experiences, viewpoints, and feelings. Show them that you genuinely understand and value where they're coming from.

Let go of any expectations you may have regarding their emotional response.

Remember, forgiveness and trust can't be forced or rushed. Healing takes time and patience. It's completely normal for hurt feelings to show up as anger, distance, or not caring. Just keep staying committed to the healing process and be patient, even when things get tough.

Make a conscious effort to prioritize your child.

Take the initiative to plan activities that they will enjoy, whether it's watching a favorite TV show or movie together or engaging in a game of cards. Remember not to force their participation but instead extend a genuine invitation.

Show your support by attending their events whenever possible. If you have scheduling limitations, communicate with them and inquire about the events at which they would most like you to be present. By actively participating in their lives and being there for important moments, you demonstrate your love and commitment to their happiness.

Share with your kids as much as is appropriate. Be open and honest.

Be open with your child about their experience and anything outside their experience that they may not know. Share what is appropriate. If you are responsible for any part of it, take responsibility for your actions. Look ahead to the future, sharing how you intend to help them recover from the trauma. And if needed, how you will do things differently in the future. If necessary, make a list of the changes that need to occur.

Ask for forgiveness.

If you are responsible for any part, then apologize. Even if you were unable to control the situation or help at the time. Remember their experience is different from yours. For example, we apologized to our daughter for not being there to protect her. Of course, we couldn't help it, but in her mind, we are her parents and should have been there.

When you apologize for your mistakes, make sure it comes from the heart and is genuine. A sincere apology is backed up by a commitment to change behavior. Explain to your child, in words they can understand, why you're seeking forgiveness and what you're apologizing for. Be honest and straightforward, letting them know that you're taking responsibility for your actions and that you're committed to making things right.

Address the changes you will make.

If changes need to be made, be clear with your child about the specific changes you intend to make and how you'll make them happen. You can even jot down a list if it helps you remember what needs to change. By sharing your plans for improvement, you demonstrate your commitment to a better future and assure your child that positive changes are on the way.

Let your child know that making mistakes is normal, but assure them that you won't give up. Emphasize that you're always willing to start fresh, even if it means going back to square one and having another conversation. Reassure your child that your determination to improve and grow is unwavering.

Give yourself grace.

You're not perfect, and that's okay. Mistakes will happen along the way, but what matters is your willingness to learn from them and keep trying. Don't be afraid to start over and have another conversation if needed. Give yourself grace, knowing that mistakes are opportunities for growth. Predetermine that when you stumble, you'll learn from it, do better, and continue moving forward on this journey of rebuilding trust with your child.

SELF-REFLECTION

Looking ahead, how will you prepare to support your child in dealing with potentially traumatic experiences, whether big or small? How can you create an environment where they feel safe and secure, even when facing challenging situations?

....

....

....

....

....

....

....

EMOTIONAL RESPONSES

Parenting a child who has experienced trauma can be a difficult process, but with patience and intentionality, we help rebuild our child's confidence and create healthy family boundaries. There will be some bumps along the road, but as parents, we can create a safe haven where our children can heal and thrive. It's through these ups and downs that we not only rebuild our child's confidence but also reinforce our family bonds. In the end, we're building a foundation of love and resilience that can withstand whatever comes our way.

EMOTIONAL DYSREGULATION

When kids experience trauma, their emotional regulation system can be disrupted. Emotional Dysregulation is when a child experiences complications or difficulty with registering emotions, responding with emotions that are appropriate to the context, and regulating emotional responses in social settings. These children often find it hard to control emotions or have excessive emotional responses.

Symptoms of Emotional Dysregulation in children may include:[1]

- Severe tantrums
- Low tolerance for frustration
- Aggression and outbursts
- Refusal to engage in expected behaviors/activities
- Frequent crying and negative moods
- Thoughts of self-harm

---

1   https://compasshealthcenter.net/specialties/dysregulation-in-children/

Effects of Emotional Dysregulation in a child's life:[2]

- Lack of interest in making new friends
- Loss of peer relationships due to outbursts
- Feelings of sadness due to uncontrolled emotional responses
- Unsatisfactory academic performance
- School refusal or avoidance
- Possibility of causing stress to other children in social settings

What You Can Do to Help:

- Recognize the triggers. Be aware when outbursts happen and try to understand what causes them.
- Reward positive behavior. When your child has a positive response or avoids a negative response, compliment the behavior. A reward system might also be beneficial.
- Be a positive role model by modeling appropriate responses to difficult situations.
- Talk about appropriate responses to our feelings and difficult situations when the child is emotionally level. Use yourself as an example rather than your child.
- Find books about feelings and read them to or with your child. Sending a message that feelings are okay and that we all have them can help your child cope with theirs.
- When your child is calm, talk about and practice different calm-down methods. It is important to practice these during calm times. A child cannot be taught when they are overwhelmed.

---

2   https://compasshealthcenter.net/specialties/dysregulation-in-children/

TRIGGERS

When we see a child, or even an adult, who loses control of his or her emotional response, then they are likely triggered by something. A trigger is something (it can be anything: a sound, a phrase, a smell, or a food) that causes the brain to remember a certain event, usually a traumatic one. When we experience a trigger, our brain takes us back to the event and we experience it as if we are there again. This can cause our brain to go into protection mode and our body to respond to the event.

I'm going to use a positive example here. Let's say you have an aunt or uncle that you spent weekends with as a child. This aunt or uncle lived on a farm. Each time you stayed you were allowed to feed the chickens. You loved staying there and seeing all the animals, helping on the farm and roasting marshmallows at night. As an adult, you might be triggered by certain farm smells or by seeing someone feeding chickens. You might find yourself suddenly caught up in your memory and feeling that warm feeling of delight from your childhood.

Triggers bring about real reactions in the present caused by past events. When a child is triggered, they might not be in control of their actions. Understanding that can help us respond appropriately.

ANGER

Anger is often a secondary emotion. When our children experience emotions like fear, shame, or disappointment, it can come out as anger. It is important to recognize that their anger is not always as simple as it seems.

Whenever anger appears in our children, we should always look beneath the surface.

The process of rebuilding trust can be a long, messy one with a lot of stops and starts. Be prepared to stick with the process even when it seems like it is not working. This is a process for starting over. This is meant to be a guideline. Adapt this process to meet the needs of your family. Whenever possible, a family counselor or other professional can be a helpful resource.

Whenever anger appears in our children, we should always look beneath the surface.

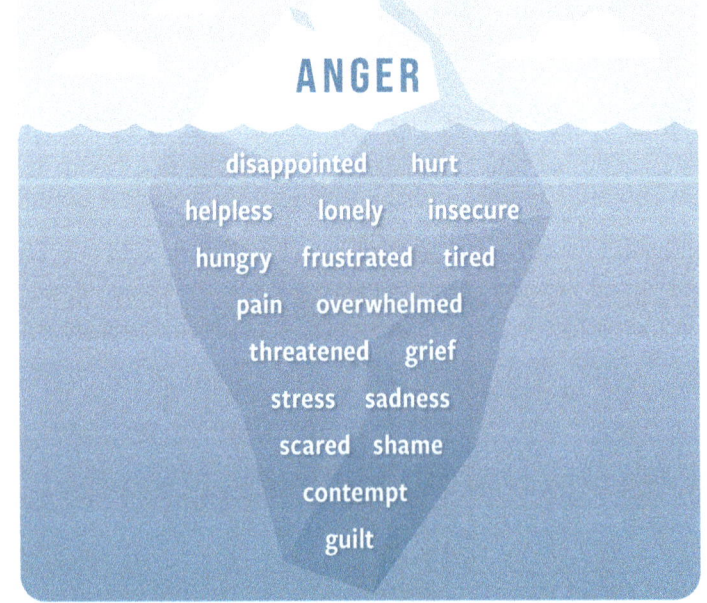

ANGER

disappointed   hurt
helpless   lonely   insecure
hungry   frustrated   tired
pain   overwhelmed
threatened   grief
stress   sadness
scared   shame
contempt
guilt

COPING STRATEGIES

Coping strategies are simple ways to help you calm down and deal with a tough situation. Everyone can use them. What works for some may not work for others. Encourage your kids to try different strategies and find what works. Have them choose one or two they like from the chart and practice using them during calm times. Continue practicing with your kids during moments of calm and soon it will become easier for them to use the strategies during moments of high emotions.

ACTIVE	CREATIVE	THOUGHTFUL	SOUND
Run in place or do 10 jumping jacks.	Color or draw a picture.	Count backwards from 10, 50, 100.	Recite a favorite song or nursery rhyme.
Play with a calming toy. Legos, blocks, etc.	Write a journal entry.	Think of your favorite TV show and focus on one episode.	Say the alphabet backward.
Take a walk or jog around the block.	List 3, 5, or 10 adjectives, verbs, states, etc.	Think of solutions to the problem at hand.	Hum your favorite song or tune.
Follow a finger-tapping pattern over and over until you don't mess up.	Write an acrostic poem about a friend or family member. (Each letter of their name starts a word)	Think of feeling words and put them in the category of either LOUD or QUIET.	Say out loud 3 things you can see, 2 things you can hear, and 1 thing you can touch.
Ask for help or talk to a friend.	Make up a game for frogs.	Phone a friend and say, "Right now I feel..."	Say the Pledge of Allegiance in a foreign accent.
Play a card or board game.	Think of a rule or law you would change. Figure out how you would make it happen.	Think of problems you have solved in the past. Keep a running list.	Be still and listen and name the sounds you hear.

As your child grows, how will you encourage them to explore and choose coping strategies that work best for their unique needs? Can you envision specific Snapshots where they might successfully apply these strategies to manage challenging moments?

....

....

....

....

....

....

....

AUTHORITY AND TRUST

When we are in the process of restoring trust with our children, it can create a sticky situation when it comes to our authority. As we have learned, our children often have emotional responses as a result of their trauma. As parents, it can be difficult for us to hold boundaries when we feel responsible in some way for their past trauma. As the parent we have authority, but as we recover and rebuild relationships, we might feel like we have given up our right to that authority.

Regardless of how we feel about it, we have a responsibility to guide, equip, and protect our children.

FEELINGS VS. ACTIONS

Understanding the difference between feelings and actions can help us navigate the uncertain territory of parenting while rebuilding trust. It is okay for our kids to get angry or upset. Those are their feelings. It is not okay for our kids to act out because of their feelings. Actions can be controlled, and we should teach our kids how to control their actions even when they are feeling big emotions. For children who have experienced trauma, controlling their actions during big, emotional moments will be more difficult. Patience and consistency are important when it comes to helping a child cope with the effects of trauma.

Our children might have negative feelings toward us and that's okay. We can respect their feelings and give them room to explore and process them. However, their feelings do not give them the right to act any way they choose. Regardless of our mistakes, we are their parents, and we must set healthy boundaries for their good. We have a responsibility to hold those boundaries as well.

Our job is to teach our children the difference between feelings and actions. Using patience and understanding, we have to help our children understand that while they can be angry or upset with us, their situation, or anything, they cannot act in any way they choose. Using this explanation along with the principle of holding boundaries can help us navigate these difficult situations.

We must set healthy boundaries for the good of our children.

↓ FINAL THOUGHTS

Parenting children who have experienced trauma can be a deeply challenging journey. Traumatic experiences often create challenges that can last for years and can manifest in various ways, impacting a child's emotional, psychological, and behavioral well-being. While our children face difficulties like trust, self-regulation, and forming secure attachments, they depend on us to create a safe space as they heal. As difficult as this might be, the challenge is even more difficult when we are responsible for or involved with the trauma.

The path to healing for our children often requires a heightened level of patience, empathy, and understanding from us. Building a safe and nurturing environment, creating consistent routines, and providing access to mental health professionals can help our children develop healthier coping mechanisms and work through their trauma. With time, love, and professional assistance, we can help our children rebuild their sense of security, trust, and self-worth, and we can rebuild healthy relationships within our families.

↓ THINK AND DISCUSS

Considering the topics we have covered in this chapter, reflect on the following Snapshots. If you are in a group setting, take some time to discuss them with each other. Remember that there is not always a single right or wrong answer. There are many considerations and perspectives to explore, so embrace the opportunity for critical thinking and meaningful conversations that broaden your understanding.

IN THIS CHAPTER, WE DISCUSSED

- Trust Broken in Big and Small Ways
- Emotional Dysregulation
- Coping Strategies

SNAPSHOT 1
SHOVING MATCH

Ten-year-old Matthew got into a shoving match with his teammate, Jackson, during his baseball game. Unknown to Matthew's parents, Adam and Priscilla, Jackson has been making rude comments to Matthew during the games. Jackson also invited every teammate to his birthday party, except Matthew.

→ **QUESTIONS TO CONSIDER**

1. Is there an underlying emotion or root cause?

2. How would the 3C approach to discipline apply here?

3. Moving forward, how can Adam and Priscilla use feelings vs. actions to equip Matthew to better deal with situations like this?

4. Consider your own children. What coping strategies might help in this situation?

SNAPSHOT 2
STRUGGLING AT HOME

Fourteen-year-old Caroline experienced an extremely traumatic event at home, followed by spending a year with a foster family. She has recently been reunited with her parents, Jason and Charlotte. Her foster parents were very caring and understanding. They stayed in touch with Caroline's parents and worked with them to parent her so that her life was disrupted in the least amount possible. After being home for a few months, Caroline struggles to get back into the routine of going to school. She often refuses to get ready in the mornings. She seems to be intentionally trying to make herself late for school.

→ **QUESTIONS TO CONSIDER**

1. How might have spending a year with foster parents been traumatic for Caroline?

2. How can Jason and Charlotte rebuild trust with Caroline?

3. Understanding emotional dysregulation, how can Caroline's parents help her navigate this?

FAMILY RESET GUIDE

FAMILY RESET

The first step in fostering change is to take an honest look at ourselves.

Sometimes, we will find ourselves overwhelmed by the amount of arguing, repeating ourselves, bribing, and giving in we do just to keep the peace. You may have read this book and feel like you are starting too late or it would be impossible to change anything now. Your children have basically taken over and you are held captive by their emotions and controlled by their tantrums. When we find ourselves here, it can create a feeling of desperation or defeat.

But I want to encourage you in this season—things can improve, and a Family Reset is a great place to start. The goal of the Family Reset is to break the cycles of negative habits and behavior and start putting healthy ones in place, creating a more peaceful atmosphere in your home. This chapter will guide you toward that goal.

The Family Reset is broken up into five steps. As you read through each step, take the time to consider each section and reflect on your own experiences and how the strategies presented can be applied to your unique family dynamics. At the end of each step, you'll find action steps. These are questions and prompts designed to help you tailor these strategies to best fit your circumstances.

STEP ONE: EXAMINE OURSELVES

The first step in fostering change is to take an honest look at ourselves. This can be difficult because we want so much to be the best parents for our children and when we consider the possibility that we might not be, it can be devastating. The fact is, however, that we all have opportunities to grow. When we are willing to hold a mirror up to ourselves, identify these areas, and work toward making positive changes, we are setting a powerful example for our children. We are modeling self-reflection and accountability.

Through this process, we teach our children that it's not only okay but also admirable to recognize our imperfections and actively strive to improve. By demonstrating the value of self-awareness and the ability to change, we empower our children to face their own challenges and setbacks with resilience and a growth mindset. This pivotal step not only benefits our own parenting journey but also paves the way for a healthier, more harmonious family dynamic.

It is important to understand that any change we want to see in our children starts with us. Before we can start making changes within our family dynamics, especially behavioral changes, we need to reflect. This means that we will have to take a long look in the mirror and dig into our own issues.

OUR UNMET NEEDS

Sometimes, we as parents can have emotional needs that we are unaware of. Without realizing it, we place the burden of those needs on our kids, creating an unhealthy dynamic in the relationship and the home. As parents, we must work to understand our own needs and emotions and find a healthy way to meet those needs so they don't negatively affect our actions and decision-making.

When we are unaware of our unmet emotional needs, we can unknowingly create unfair expectations that our kids know nothing about. Parenting from our emotions is like asking our children to walk through a minefield. They never know when they are going to cause an explosion.

When we snap at our kids, we should stop and ask ourselves why we are responding this way. What are we really responding to? Often we will find that it is because our child has hit a nerve, which is a strong sign that there is an unmet need there. When we understand our emotional needs, we can be more aware of when we are expecting our kids to meet those needs.

While not a comprehensive list, the following examples are some of the most common emotional needs that parents place on their children: control, validation, respect, and security.

The Need for Control

This is a widespread need, and it's natural to want control over our lives. When we can't control our kids' growing personalities and desires, some of us may start exerting control over them. This can undermine their ability to self-regulate and accept responsibility. Instead of learning to manage their behavior, our children may become reactive and rebellious, pushing back against excessive control.

Constantly parenting from a need for control is a habit that needs to be broken. When we control our kids, we take away their ability to learn and grow into themselves. Managing and controlling every aspect of our children's lives can leave them feeling resentful and lead to rebellion as they get older.

God has created each of us for His purpose, and that includes our children. While we do need to establish our authority when our children are younger, ask yourself these questions. If any of them ring true, you might be parenting from a need for control.

- Do I make most of the decisions for my child, including the insignificant ones?
- Do I "help" my child without being asked?
- Do I get upset when my child doesn't do things my way or "the right way" even when they accomplish the goal?
- Do I use guilt or emotions to make my child do what I want?

The Need for Validation

There are two aspects to the need for validation. The first is when we seek validation directly from our children. The second aspect is when we seek validation from their behavior. Regardless of where the tendency to seek validation leans, parents who have this need tend to focus on the opinions of others to define their worth or value. And with that tendency, consciously or not, we teach our children to seek success and approval as a means of validating their self-worth and cripple their ability to find joy in their hard work and effort.

We all want to be validated sometimes but seeking it from our children can leave them feeling responsible for us and our wellbeing. Seeking validation from their behavior can leave them feeling the need to perform in order to please us. Ask yourself these questions and if any of them ring true, you might be parenting from a need for validation.

- Am I snapping at my kids because they are behaving in a way that makes me look bad?
- Do I get stressed out about how my kids will make me look in front of others?
- Do I focus more on trying to make my kids behave in front of others?
- Am I constantly ending my requests with "okay?" or "Is that okay?"
- Am I trying to please my children and keep them happy?
- Am I constantly looking for signs that my child accepts me as a parent, a friend, or a person?

The Need to Feel Respected

Respect is something many of us desire, but the way we define respect varies. When we parent from a need to be respected, we might set unspoken rules that can change with our mood or daily experiences. This can lead to misunderstandings, as children unintentionally violate these ever-shifting rules.

The need to be respected is a feeling-based need, which is different from a general expectation of treating people with respect. When we set an expectation that we treat others with respect, we can clearly define those boundaries and explain what they look like. When we parent from a need to be respected, there are no clear boundaries because the definition of respect changes with our feelings and moods. We may not even fully understand it ourselves. We just know that sometimes we suddenly feel angry and lash out when our children respond to us.

Ask yourself these questions. If any of them ring true, you might be parenting from a need for respect.

- Do I get angry or agitated when I feel like my child is challenging my authority?
- Do I react harshly when my child talks back in front of others?
- Does my child appear hurt or confused when I accuse them of disrespecting me?

The Need for Security

The need for security often stems from our fears, such as concerns about our children's safety, success, and financial stability, or even the fear that our kids might repeat our mistakes. While these fears are common, parenting from a place of fear can cause children to adopt these fears as their own.

Parenting from a need for security can come in several forms. Sometimes it can be difficult to recognize because we feel like we are protecting our children. However, it is important to be self-aware as we learn and grow. Take some time to evaluate yourself. Ask yourself these questions. If any of them ring true, you might be parenting from a need for security.

- Do I often predict a negative outcome in a certain area?
- Do I often tell my kids no based on the possibility of harm?
- Do I focus more on keeping my kids from making mistakes than helping them overcome when they do?

ONE THING TO NOTE

Parenting from immediate needs is not inherently negative. Sometimes, we need peaceful moments or quick resolutions. However, it's crucial to stay reflective and identify patterns. If your immediate needs frequently dictate your parenting style, it may be time to break those patterns. Nonetheless, there are instances where asserting your needs as a parent is entirely reasonable. For example, if you need quiet to talk to a plumber, or you simply can't handle a messy baking session, it's your prerogative to make those calls as a parent.

ACTION STEPS

Consider the following questions carefully, and take the time to reflect on yourself and your role in the family dynamic. If possible, write your answers in the space provided.

1. Have you ever felt overwhelmed by arguments, repeating yourself, or giving in to your children? How do you typically handle these situations?

....

....

....

....

....

....

....

....

2. Can you recall instances when your emotional responses to your children's behavior were strong indicators of unmet needs? What were these situations?

....

....

....

....

....

....

....

....

STEP TWO: IDENTIFY BEHAVIORS

When we find ourselves overwhelmed with our children's behaviors or the entire family dynamic, it can be difficult to understand what is really going on. Take the time to sort through it all and identify the root causes of these challenges. By doing so, we can gain a deeper comprehension of the underlying issues that contribute to the chaos and turmoil in our family life.

It's important to distinguish between genuinely inappropriate behaviors and those that are merely bothersome or age-appropriate. Not every behavior requires immediate intervention or correction. Inappropriate behaviors are those that are not in line with family or societal norms or that go against specific family boundaries. These may include lying, stealing, being disrespectful, or outright defiance. It's vital to address inappropriate behaviors promptly.

On the other hand, some behaviors are more of a nuisance, such as constant arguing, sibling rivalry, or messy rooms. While these can be frustrating, they don't necessarily pose significant risks. Differentiating between the two types of behaviors allows us to prioritize our efforts, ensuring that we address potentially detrimental behaviors more urgently and approach others with patience and guidance.

As we consider the negative behaviors we are witnessing in our children, we should be aware of the potential deep-rooted causes. Are they the result of our own actions? For example, when our kids are younger, we might give in to their tantrums in order to have peace. As they get older, it becomes more difficult to meet their demands, and their tantrums escalate. There is a big difference between the tantrum of a three-year-old and one thrown by a twelve-year-old.

It is also important to consider whether a specific incident or circumstance led to the behavior. Before you deal with behaviors, make sure there is no underlying issue or struggle within your child. Often our children act out because they want attention or they have no other way to express themselves.

My younger daughter suddenly started refusing to go to school. She would say she had a stomachache, which she did, and beg to stay home. It seemed at first that this behavior was rebellious. However, the more we investigated, we realized that she had witnessed a classmate vomit. This caused her to fear that she might also throw up in class. The more she thought about it, the more anxious she became. Her stomach began to hurt, which caused the fear to get stronger. When we realized that we were not dealing with defiant behavior, we changed our approach and sought help for her. With the help of a professional, she was able to identify and work through her anxious thoughts.

My daughter had experienced trauma. Though it might seem insignificant to us, and even to her classmates, to her it was very significant. With no tools to process this event, her emotional response system went into flight mode. She did her best to avoid having the same thing happen to her.

Some behaviors will be like the ones my daughter exhibited. They come from our children's emotional response system. For these types of behaviors, it is important to find the root cause of the behavior. It is also important to get help when we don't understand the behaviors or how to help our children.

Other behaviors are due to a lack of parental consistency. We might have ignored our children's behaviors when they were young, allowing a habit to form. Or we responded to certain behaviors in a way that reinforced them. Take a moment to create a list of the behaviors that you want to work on with your child. Also, take some time to investigate possible causes of the behavior(s).

Choose One Behavior

An essential part of resetting is focusing on one thing at a time. If there are several behaviors you want to work on, decide which one you want to address first. When we try to change too much at one time, we end up making little progress. This is why we often find ourselves correcting our children all day for the same handful of behaviors. When we have no plan, we are inconsistent in how and why we correct our children, most likely with our correction directly correlating with our moods.

By working on one behavior at a time, we can remain focused on that behavior and correct it every time. This single-focused correction has several benefits. It relieves us of the pressure to correct everything all the time. It relieves our children of the pressure to get everything right all the time. It allows everyone to be on the same page. When there is a single focus and a single plan it is also easier for parenting partners to be united. It allows us to be more consistent, which is the key to helping our children relearn the correct behaviors.

ACTION STEPS

1. List the negative behaviors that you have observed in your children. If possible, do so in the space provided.

   ....
   ....
   ....
   ....

2. Consider the root of those behaviors. Differentiate between the inappropriate behaviors and those that are age-appropriate. Write any notes or thoughts you have in the space below.

   ....
   ....
   ....
   ....

3. If you've identified several behaviors you'd like to address, which one are you most comfortable starting with, and why? Write your answer here.

   ....
   ....
   ....
   ....

STEP THREE: DECIDE THE COURSE OF ACTION

Predetermining our actions makes it easier for us to follow through later. When we decide that we are going to address negative behaviors in our child, making a plan ahead of time will create more room for success as we get into the process. By setting clear expectations and consequences in advance, we not only provide consistency for our child but also give ourselves the confidence needed to address these behaviors effectively. This pre-planned approach allows us to focus on one behavior at a time, ensuring we can implement the plan consistently and increase the likelihood of positive outcomes.

The plan follows three stages: reminding, redirecting, and correcting. The reminding stage is simply reminding our children that we are working on the behavior each time we see it. Redirecting adds the element of change. We have our child replace the negative behavior with an acceptable one. Correcting comes in if we see that our child is continuing to willfully express the behavior. At this point, we implement the predetermined consequence.

Think about how you will respond to the behavior when it happens. A predetermined response will help decrease negative reactions. Remember, a response considers the well-being of the child and all involved.

Our response should be in line with the behavior. If our child is telling us no, grounding them for a week each time would not be in line with the behavior. More serious behaviors might need a more serious response. Be sure that whatever you decide, you can stay consistent. Our children are often happy to go along with our plans while we are the ones who struggle to keep up with them. The following questions will help you come up with an appropriate response that you can use with your child.

- Will there be consequences?
- Will I use redirection?
- What will my verbal response be?
- How will I respond if we are in public?
- Will there be rewards? Will there be goals to hit?

ACTION STEPS

Keeping in mind that the goal is to set your child up for success. Consider the consequences, redirection strategies, verbal responses, and potential rewards for the behavior you're targeting. Decide which strategies will work best for your child as well as your lifestyle.

Reminding

Write down a reminder phrase. Remember the PBS model (polite, behavior-focused, simple). *Example: Remember this is the behavior we talked about. Being disrespectful is not okay.*

....

....

....

....

Redirecting

Add a redirection aspect to your reminder phrase. *Example: Remember we are working on being polite, even when we are upset. Try again, please.*

....

....

....

....

Reinforcing

If consequences become necessary, how will you implement them? Consider different Snapshots in which the behavior occurs. How will the consequences work within them?

....

....

....

....

STEP FOUR: DRAFT A CONVERSATION

Starting with a conversation when implementing the Family Reset is important. Healthy conversation promotes open communication and transparency within your family. It will allow you to explain your need for change and how these changes will benefit your family as a whole. Conversations also provide a springboard for change. Anytime we want to make a significant change within our families, a conversation is a good way to make that transition.

Including your child in the discussion will foster a sense of involvement and shared responsibility, making them more receptive to the process. Be sure to allow your children to express their opinions, feelings, and concerns. This not only validates their perspectives but will also help you gain insight into your child's mindset, making it easier to tailor the plan to the specific needs of the family. Starting with a conversation sets a positive tone for the journey ahead, emphasizing collaboration and mutual understanding as key components of the transformation.

Once you have thought it through, it is time to bring your child in through conversation. They may be a little shocked at this point, especially if you have never done anything like this. Remember that even if the goal is to correct their behaviors, allowing them to be heard will set the stage for a more collaborative experience.

Drafting your conversation, or some key points, ahead of time will help you stay on track during the talk.

ACTION STEPS

Use the following prompts to make some notes and prepare for a conversation with your child or your family.

Start with a positive.

What is great about your child(ren) and your family? Begin with some positive thoughts. Be authentic about the positive attributes you see in your child and your family.

....

....

....

....

What needs to change?

Start by explaining that things need to change, and the change will be better for the whole family. Consider your positives from the last prompt. Will changes help maintain those positives?

....

....

....

....

Explain the behavior/behaviors that need to change and why. Be sure to include that the behaviors don't fit the character of your child.

....

....

....

....

How will we change?

Explain how the plan will work. Include the reminding, redirecting, and reinforcing steps.

....

....

....

....

Explain what you will do differently going forward. How will you help your child be successful?

....

....

....

....

Check for understanding.

Ask your child to tell you in their own words what they have heard. Go back over anything that they have misunderstood. Having something in writing can be a great way to keep everyone accountable. This is important to avoid confusion when the time comes to implement consequences.

STEP FIVE: IMPLEMENT THE PLAN

As you start addressing the targeted behavior, rely on the three key stages of *reminding*, *redirecting*, and *reinforcing* to provide guidance and structure. The reminding stage helps bring awareness of the behavior to your child's mind, while the redirecting stage offers an opportunity for your child to replace the negative behavior with a positive one. Finally, the reinforcing stage, though implemented with empathy and understanding, utilizes consequences that are applied consistently. Consistency and patience are your allies as you work through this transformation, reducing chaos and creating a more harmonious family environment.

When the first behavior has been eliminated, move to the next one. After addressing the first behavior, however, you might find that other behaviors seem to take care of themselves. Once our children understand that we are going to stick to our guns, they will likely begin to adjust accordingly. This is a result of the re-establishment of our authority. Our children need clear boundaries and a strong authority to enforce them. As the parent-child dynamic is brought into balance and boundaries are consistently enforced, our children will gradually understand the importance of adhering to these expectations. It's a natural response to the re-establishment of our authority, creating a more structured and stable family environment.

Reminding

Just like adults, it takes time for our children to unlearn negative habits and replace them with positive ones. So we use reminding and redirecting to give our children a chance to do that. When we see the behavior, we remind our children (using our predetermined phrase if necessary) that this is the behavior we are working on.

Redirecting

When we feel that our children are ready, we can add redirecting. When we notice the behavior, we remind our child of it then redirect them or have them replace the behavior with a positive new one. As we redirect our children, we are giving them the opportunity to replace the old behavior with a new one. This is an important part of helping them change negative behaviors.

Correcting

We must be consistent during this phase, implementing consequences every time. At this point, you are showing your child that you are serious and the behavior must change. Interestingly, when parents implement this plan, they often find that the other behaviors fall away naturally.

ACTION STEP

It's time to put it all in place. Find a good time for a talk and use your conversation guide to get the ball rolling. Once you feel confident that your child understands, it will be time to move forward. Remember that consistency is a key part of the success.

FINAL THOUGHTS

When the parent-child dynamic is out of balance and boundaries are inconsistently enforced, it can lead to confusion, frustration, and misbehavior. By consistently addressing and correcting negative behaviors, your children will recognize the authority that provides them with a sense of security and clear expectations. This positive shift will likely result in an overall improvement in your children's behaviors, fostering a healthier and more peaceful family life. This can all seem overwhelming at first. Making changes like this can be a lot of work, but this plan will help you break it into manageable, focused steps. Remember why you are here in the first place. Go back to the beginning if you need to and consider the cost of not making changes. In the moment, it can feel more doable to let things be and ride it out. But we are not parenting for right now. We are parenting for the future. Putting in the hard work right now will pay off in peace and order in the home later.

Go ahead and commit to following through. This means settling in your mind that this could take a while. If you are at this point, then these behaviors have probably been going on for a while. So, it will take time to form new habits and behaviors. This could take a month or two. Accept it and be consistent—the payoff will be worth it!

↓ THINK AND DISCUSS

This chapter is a bit different from the others in that it takes you through a plan of action. For this Think and Discuss, there aren't any snapshots to consider because you probably already have your own real-life scenarios to consider. So the questions here will help you reflect on your plan and seek and offer encouragement to others.

IN THIS CHAPTER, WE DISCUSSED

- Reflecting on our unmet needs
- Identifying negative behaviors
- Talking to our children
- Reminding, Redirecting, and Correcting

→ QUESTIONS TO CONSIDER

1. Do you find yourself parenting from any unmet needs? What can you do to help yourself meet those needs?

2. After reflecting on your child(ren)'s behaviors, have you identified any outside circumstances that might be causing the behavior? If so, how will you address it?

3. Talk about the laser focus on a single behavior. Why is it important? How can you deal with other behaviors that are not the focus?

4. What is the point of the reminding, redirecting and correcting process? How will you apply it within your family?

BEFORE YOU GO...

Parenting is a lifelong commitment, filled with joys and challenges. There will be days when you feel overwhelmed, uncertain, or even exhausted. But I want to remind you of something crucial: you are doing an amazing job. Each day that you pour your love, energy, and wisdom into your children, you are creating a foundation of trust and connection that will last a lifetime.

Remember, parenting is not about perfection; it's about progress. It's about embracing the imperfections and turning them into opportunities for growth. Our mistakes are not failures, but valuable lessons that guide us towards becoming better parents. Embrace these lessons with grace, knowing that the love and effort you invest in your children far outweigh any missteps along the way.

Throughout this book, we have discovered the power of communication, empathy, and active listening in fostering deep connections with our children. Continue to create spaces where your children feel safe to express themselves, where their voices are heard and their emotions acknowledged. These bonds will be the foundation from which they learn to navigate relationships and thrive in their own lives.

Don't forget to celebrate the small victories and milestones. These years with your children will be filled with countless moments that shape your family's story. Cherish them. Embrace the laughter, the hugs, the tears, and all the experiences that fill your days. Take time to appreciate the unique qualities and strengths your children possess, nurturing their individuality and supporting their dreams. Remember, your presence and unwavering support are the greatest gifts you can give them.

I want you to know that you are not alone on this journey. Seek out support, whether it be from friends, family, or parenting communities. Share your experiences, exchange advice, and find encouragement in knowing that others have faced similar challenges. Together, we can build a network of support that uplifts and strengthens all families.

Finally, thank you for allowing me to be a part of your parenting journey. It is an honor and a privilege to share insights and guidance with you as you navigate the beautiful and challenging path of raising your children. I am grateful for the opportunity to support and inspire you along the way. Your dedication and love as a parent are truly remarkable, and I am thankful to be a small part of your family's story.

ACKNOWLEDGEMENTS

Writing a book is a lot like parenting. You think you know what you're doing until you find yourself face-to-face with a blank page. I cannot tell you how many hours I've spent staring at a computer screen trying to figure out what to say. I love to talk about parenting, whether that's through teaching classes, leading small groups, or talking with moms over coffee. Writing about it is another animal. So, to write this book, I did a lot of praying. Then I started talking about it by teaching it. I began teaching classes using just the topics and the outlines. Knowing I had a class each week, I would write the material for that week's topic. As I taught, the book began to take shape. Then, another shape. And another. And yet another. Changing and shifting until I finally felt like it was something I could share with the world.

I am so thankful for Melinda and Joseph at The Lovelady Center for allowing me to share my thoughts and ideas about parenting with their precious mothers. I am also grateful to the Lovelady moms who are so gracious, allowing me to share my heart with them and sharing theirs with me in return. I have had some of the best conversations in the classes I have taught there. In fact, it was out of that service that I founded Seeds of Impact.

I've always romanticized the book-writing process. I imagined days spent away at some exotic location looking out the window at some magnificent view as the words flowed onto the page. Sure, there were days away courtesy of the generosity of my family. I've been fortunate to spend time writing at my mother-in-law's lake house. I am writing this while sitting at my sister's beach house on St. George Island in Florida and feeling a little *Hilderbrandesque*. I treasure those times, and they helped me produce the meat of this book.

In reality, the book-writing process reminds me so much of parenting. Don't we romanticize it before we know better? Before we are plunged into it head first, walking out of the hospital terrified that someone will stop us (and secretly wishing they would)? I have realized that the writing process looks nothing like I dreamed it would. Most of my writing has been done on the sofa in my living room or at coffee shops. Finding an hour here and there—usually before anyone else wakes up—to draft a few paragraphs or read and edit a chapter. Searching for ideas I wrote down somewhere at some point. Writing this book has been messy and chaotic, but I like it that way. Because my topic, parenting, can be messy and chaotic, it weirdly makes me feel connected.

I have always wondered what it would be like to work with an editor, and thanks to mine, Andrew, I am happy to report it is a fabulously chaotic process. He has not only edited but also walked me through the writing and publishing process, making sure I felt comfortable with each step.

I am thankful for those who have helped me along the way. My mom has encouraged me in my parenting as well as my writing. She has read and reread many of the words in this book, offering insights and helping me shape it into what it is today. My two best friends, Tiffanie and Kristen, have always been there to provide encouragement, wisdom, support, truth, and, most of all, unconditional love. If you are lucky enough to find friends like these two, cherish them. Cindy, my friend and mentor, shared her time and wisdom, helping me to grow as a mom, a follower of Christ, and a person. My precious friend, Jessica, led group after group of moms to test this book. Thank you for constantly building me up and cheering me on. For those who, like Anna, Marnie, and Antoinette, have fielded random questions and requests (usually out of the blue) throughout this process, I love that you get the process. I am so thankful for the people God has placed on my path and in my life.

I try to parent like I preach, but as most parents know, it's not always that easy. There is no feeling quite like the imposter syndrome you experience when you find yourself failing at the very thing you are trying to teach others how to do. (And I have failed a lot as a parent.) I am far from perfect, and I am grateful to my husband and daughters for their grace and understanding and for encouraging me as a "parenting expert." The great thing about my family is that they are honest and grace-filled, and I need both. I am thankful for Brent, who has trusted me with our kids and allowed me the room to lead our parenting journey, even when it has taken him to unfamiliar territory. Thank you for also taking the lead when necessary. I have relished being a mother to my daughters, Katelyn, who made me feel like an amazing mother, and Sarah, who helped me see that I had much to learn. Without them, I wouldn't have a book, but I also could not have become the mom that I am. They are my reason.

Like parenting, writing is a very personal and isolating job, but it takes a village to succeed—I am thankful for mine.

ABOUT THE AUTHOR

Rachel Gunn is a follower of Christ, a wife and mom, and a parent educator with a Master's in Education and a decade of teaching experience. She founded Seeds of Impact, a nonprofit through which she channels her passion for parenting and education into supporting parents, especially moms overcoming trauma and addiction. Her unique insights derived from a rich background as an educator and mother offer practical guidance to those navigating the complex landscape of modern parenting. Rachel takes great joy in empowering families with research-backed tools and a compassionate approach, making her a driving force for positive change in parenting dynamics. When not adventuring with her husband and two daughters, she can be found writing, speaking, drinking coffee, or looking for ways to avoid cooking dinner.

Connect with Rachel and see what she's up to at www.rachelgunn.com.

ABOUT SEEDS OF IMPACT

Through generational patterns and habits and a lack of resources and community, many parents find themselves repeating the same parenting techniques they experienced as kids, passing down unhealthy views of parenting and family relationships. Parents must be introduced to new ideas about parenting, empowered to make change, and believe that change is not only beneficial but possible.

Seeds of Impact is a nonprofit agency providing parenting education and support programs for parents in Greater Birmingham, Alabama. Our goal is to educate and equip parents with a healthy parenting mindset and the skills to foster healthy family relationships.

Through partnerships with local ministries and nonprofits, we provide parenting resources like *Impact Parenting* and free parenting classes and help meet various community parenting needs. These efforts can help parents break adverse generational cycles, form a healthy perspective regarding the role of parenting, and positively impact future generations. With the right tools and a healthy mindset, parents can commit the time and energy necessary to prepare their children for a positive future.

LEARN MORE ABOUT SEEDS OF IMPACT

www.seedsofimpact.org
Email hello@seedsofimpact.org
Facebook: @seedsofimpact.al
Instagram: @seedsofimpact.al

SEEDS OF
IMPACT

A portion of the proceeds from each book sold supports under-resourced parents through Seeds of Impact.

↳ OUR MISSION

Break cycles. Impact generations.

↳ OUR VISION

We will help parents break the cycle of brokenness in families, strengthen the family unit, and positively impact future generations.

↳ OUR PROGRAMS

**Parenting Classes
Community Groups
Free Parenting Resources
Community Events
Family Coaching**

Printed in the USA
CPSIA information can be obtained
at www.ICGtesting.com
CBHW081157090924
14022CB00010B/342

9 798990 952201